THE SIMON AND SCHUSTER ILLUSTRATED ENCYCLOPEDIA

THE UNIVERSE

THE SIMON AND SCHUSTER ILLUSTRATED ENCYCLOPEDIA

THE UNIVERSE

BY JAMES MUIRDEN

LITTLE SIMON
PUBLISHED BY SIMON & SCHUSTER, INC.
NEW YORK

Copyright © 1987 by Grisewood
& Dempsey Ltd

All rights reserved including the
right of reproduction in whole or
in part in any form
Published by Little Simon
A Division of Simon & Schuster,
Inc.
Simon & Schuster Building
Rockefeller Center
1230 Avenue of the Americas
New York, New York 10020
Originally published in Great
Britain by Grisewood & Dempsey
Ltd., 1987
LITTLE SIMON and colophon are
trademarks of Simon & Schuster,
Inc.
Manufactured in Hong Kong
Printed and Bound by South
China Printing Company
10 9 8 7 6 5 4 3 2 1
Library of Congress Cataloging in
Publication Data

Muirden, James.
  The universe.

  (The Simon and Schuster
illustrated encyclopedia)
  "A Little Simon book."
  Summary: Text and illustrations
provide information about the
sun, planets, stars, galaxies,and
other aspects of the universe.
Includes charts, maps, and fact
and data panels.
  1. Astronomy – Juvenile
literature. [1. Astronomy]
I. Title. II. Series.
QB46.M95   1988   520
87-20531
ISBN 0-671-64493-9

Contents

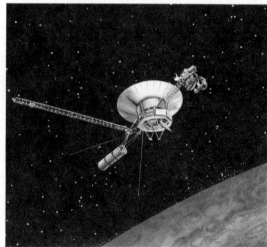

Introduction

We live on a ball of iron and rock. This ball, our planet Earth, has been whirling around a star we call the Sun for four and a half billion years. Such a long time is beyond anybody's imagination, but if you pretend that this is equal to one day, then the whole of recorded human history is equal to about a fiftieth of a second.

The Earth belongs to the **solar system** — a group of planets, **comets**, and other small objects circling the Sun. The Sun is just one of a hundred billion stars in a vast star city, which is our **Galaxy**, and there are billions of other similar galaxies in the **universe.**

Thinking about these huge numbers may make you feel very small and lonely. Certainly our planet is a very small part of the universe — but are you right to feel lonely? Hundreds of years ago, people believed that the Earth was at the center of the universe, and all living things were to be found here. Opinions have changed a great deal since then, and astronomers now believe that many of the countless stars known to exist have planets circling around them.

In this encyclopedia, you will travel on a journey to the known limits of the universe. In Chapter 1 you will discover how astronomers and scientists have improved our understanding of the Earth as a planet and of space beyond. Chapter 2 gives you an introduction to the solar system as a whole, and how we think it was formed. Chapter 3 describes our star the Sun, without which no life could exist on the Earth, and Chapter 4 takes a look at each planet in the solar system in turn. Chapter 5 explores the mysterious realms of the stars and **nebulas** in our Galaxy, while Chapter 6 surveys the other galaxies of space, and describes what we know about the birth and possible end of the universe.

To us, the Earth seems firm and still, but actually it is spinning around at a very high speed all the time. In fact, no one can say exactly where the Earth is in space because everything in the universe is continually moving. True, the Earth circles endlessly around the Sun — but where is the Sun? It is speeding past other stars in our Galaxy faster than any spacecraft. At the same time, the whole Galaxy is itself spinning like a wheel, and all the other galaxies are moving as well. Nothing stands still in space.

1. Finding Out

The first astronomers

In ancient times, anyone looking up at the sky probably thought that the Sun, the Moon, and the stars were controlled by the gods. The first people who thought they might be able to find out anything else about these heavenly bodies were the ancient Greeks.

The Greek astronomer Aristarchus, who lived in about 300 B.C. (or 300 years before the birth of Christ) was able to prove that the Sun is much farther away from us than the Moon. A few years later, a Greek mathematician Eratosthenes worked out the size of the Earth. But the most famous of the early astronomers was Ptolemy, who lived in about A.D. 100 (after the birth of Christ).

The first astronomers had no telescopes to help them study the skies, yet they still made important discoveries. The ancient Babylonian stone shown above was carved in 1100 B.C. It shows a crescent Moon, with the planet Venus on the left and the Sun on the right.

Using his eyes only, the Greek astronomer Claudius Ptolemy identified 1,080 stars, which he divided into 48 separate groups known as constellations.

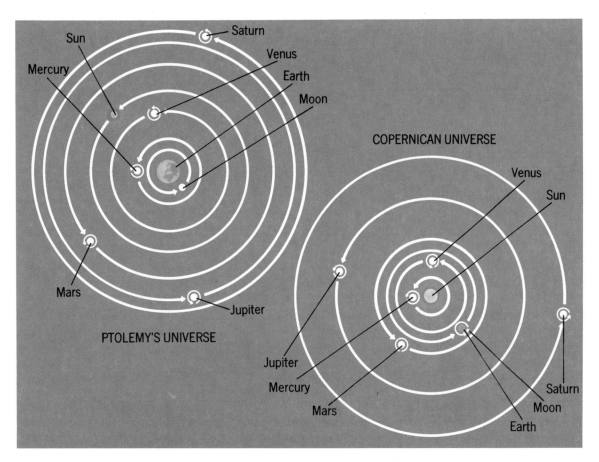

Saturn
Sun
Venus
Mercury
Earth
Moon
Mars
Jupiter

PTOLEMY'S UNIVERSE

COPERNICAN UNIVERSE

Venus
Sun
Jupiter
Mercury
Mars
Saturn
Moon
Earth

Ptolemy, like most people in those days, thought the Earth was at the center of the universe, with the Sun, Moon, planets, and stars all circling around it in their different paths or **orbits**. It was thought that all the heavenly bodies must move in circles, because the circle was the perfect shape. However, the planets did not appear to follow this perfect shape as they moved around in the sky, so Ptolemy decided that each planet also moved in a small circle or "epicycle" at the same time as it passed along its large orbit. Ptolemy worked out many strange combinations of circular whirlings until his figures matched what he could see of the real planets' movements as closely as possible.

A new idea
No one found a better method of calculating the way the planets move until 1543. This was when the Polish priest Nicolas Copernicus published a book showing that the puzzling movements of the planets could be more easily explained if they moved in circles around the Sun, not the Earth. Unfortunately, his theory made the Earth seem less important, since it was no longer the center of the universe, so many people would not accept his idea.

At that time neither the Ptolemaic nor the Copernican theory could be proved true, and both were argued over for more than half a century.

Nicolas Copernicus was educated as a priest, and made few astronomical observations, but his book, called On the Revolutions of the Heavenly Bodies, *is one of the most important ever printed.*

It is said that he touched the first printed copy just as he died.

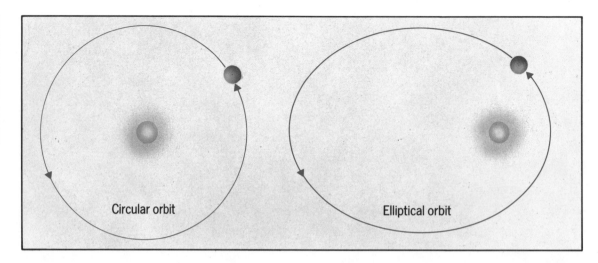

Circular orbit

Elliptical orbit

In the end, the observations which proved that the Earth and planets do orbit the Sun were made by someone who believed that Copernicus was wrong. This was the great Danish astronomer Tycho Brahe. He believed that the planets revolved around the Sun, but that the Sun circled the Earth. To try to prove this, Tycho made the best-ever "naked-eye" observations of the movements of the planets, particularly Mars.

After Tycho's death in 1601, these observations were studied by German mathematician Johann Kepler. Kepler believed in the Copernican theory and spent years trying to make Tycho's notes agree with calculations based on the Copernican model. Finally, he decided that the idea of planets moving only in circles must be wrong. He tried using an **ellipse**, and Tycho's observations fell beautifully into place.

At last it could be proved, by mathematics at least, that the Earth and planets all orbit the Sun in elliptical paths. Kepler published his great discovery in 1609, the same year that the great Italian philosopher Galileo turned his newly invented telescope to the sky.

Before Kepler's discovery, most people thought the planets moved in a circular orbit, like the one shown on the left. We now know that all bodies in space move in elliptical orbits.

An ellipse is like a flattened circle. The greater the flattening, the more "eccentric" is the ellipse. No planet has an orbit as eccentric as the one shown above, but comets' orbits may be much more eccentric than this.

DRAWING AN ELLIPSE

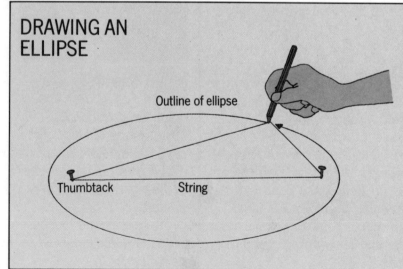

Outline of ellipse

Thumbtack   String

Stick two thumbtacks through a sheet of paper laid on a flat surface. Put a loop of thread over the pins, and draw a pencil around inside the loop, keeping it tight. See how the shape of the ellipse changes if you alter the distance between the tacks. If the ellipse were a planet's orbit, the Sun would be one of the tacks.

GALILEO – THE FIRST SCIENTIST

Galileo Galilei lived at the beginning of the 17th century. He was an outspoken man and made enemies easily, but he was also one of the first people to perform experiments to find things out. For example, most people at that time argued that any heavy weight would fall to earth more quickly than a light one, but Galileo tried dropping different weights from the same height and found out that this was not actually true.

When he heard about the invention of the telescope by a Dutch optician in 1608, Galileo immediately made his own lenses and mounted them in a tube. The moment he turned his homemade telescope to the sky, he made some sensational discoveries. He discovered that there were dark spots on the Sun, and that the planet Jupiter had four small objects orbiting around it.

People who still believed in the Ptolemaic theory refused to accept Galileo's discoveries, since they did not agree with their idea of the universe. For example, Galileo said that the planet Venus showed changing **phases** like the Moon, which meant that it had to move around the Sun and not the Earth. But Galileo's own observations convinced him that it was the Copernican Sun-centered system that was correct, not the Ptolemaic one.

Galileo was one of the first people to study the sky through a telescope. He worked from his home in Florence, Italy.

Galileo built several telescopes, but even the most powerful only enlarged or "magnified" the object he was looking at by 30 times. This telescope is the longer of the two tubes shown above. It was very awkward to use, and it is not at all surprising that others less skilled found it hard to see anything through it at all.

With his telescopes, Galileo made many discoveries, including ...

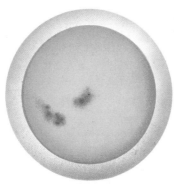

Spots on the Sun ...

Craters on the Moon ...

Objects circling Jupiter ...

The phases of Venus.

11

Windows to the stars

By the end of the 18th century, telescopes had developed from the size of Galileo's little spyglass to huge instruments higher than a house. Astronomers wanted to see the planets in more detail, and to study fainter and fainter stars. To do this, they needed telescopes of large "aperture." The aperture is the diameter of the lens or mirror that collects the light from the object being viewed and forms an image of it inside the tube.

Early telescopes did not produce a very sharp image and had apertures of only a few inches, because no one knew how to cast large pieces of glass.

But although these first telescopes seem crude compared with sleek modern instruments, the two basic types of telescopes remain the same today.

Refracting telescopes

At first, all telescopes were made in a similar fashion to Galileo's. They all used a lens, called an "object glass," to form the image. A much smaller lens, known as the "eyepiece," was fitted into the bottom of the tube to enlarge this image. This type of telescope is known as a "refracting" telescope.

However, the small aperture of these early refracting telescopes was only one of their drawbacks. The single lens in the object glass also made a false pattern of rainbow colors appear around a star or planet, making it hard to see the object clearly. This problem was not solved until 150 years after Galileo's time, when the object glass was made from two lenses close together.

The first refracting telescopes gave poor-quality images, and stars and planets appeared to be surrounded by colored halos. This color effect could be lessened if the telescope was made very long. The result was that astronomers built longer and longer telescopes. These "aerial telescopes" had to be hung on masts and were controlled by ropes. Aerial telescopes were very awkward to use, but they were the best instruments available to 17th-century astronomers.

Reflecting telescopes

Then, in 1688, the great English scientist Isaac Newton made a small telescope that used a mirror instead of a lens to form an image of the object. This type of telescope is known as a "reflecting" telescope.

Newton realized that a slightly hollowed-out or "concave" mirror could form an image just as well as a lens could. In fact, it would work better, since a mirror produces no false rainbow colors. However, the first mirrors had to be made of shiny metal, as the method of coating one side of a piece of glass with silver was unknown in those days. Metal was difficult to work with and did not reflect light very well. It was not until about 1850 that mirrors coated with highly reflective silver came into use.

Today, all large telescopes use a mirror rather than a lens, but small refracting telescopes are still popular with amateur astronomers.

Isaac Newton wrongly thought that refracting telescopes would always give a false color effect around an image. This error led him to invent the reflecting telescope!

A modern astronomical refracting telescope is like a large spyglass. It uses an "object glass," containing two lenses, to form an image of the object at the lower end of the tube. An eyepiece magnifies this image to give a close-up view of the object, and the observer looks "up" the tube.

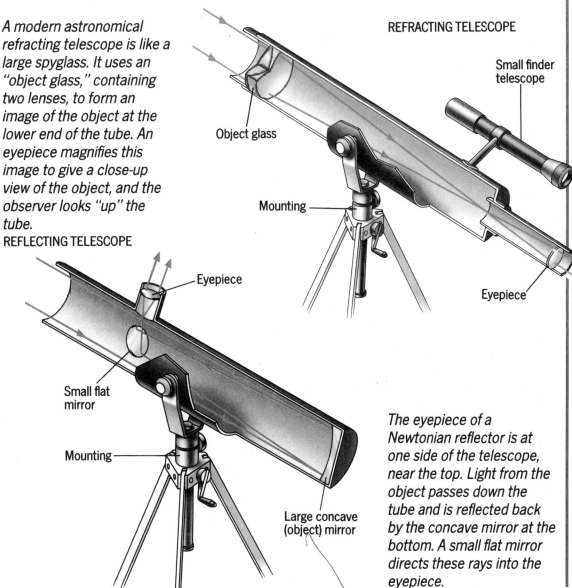

REFRACTING TELESCOPE

Small finder telescope

Object glass

Mounting

Eyepiece

REFLECTING TELESCOPE

Eyepiece

Small flat mirror

Mounting

Large concave (object) mirror

The eyepiece of a Newtonian reflector is at one side of the telescope, near the top. Light from the object passes down the tube and is reflected back by the concave mirror at the bottom. A small flat mirror directs these rays into the eyepiece.

13

Herschel discovered Uranus

... and "binary stars."

He identified many nebulas

... and star clusters.

This was Herschel's biggest telescope, and used a mirror 4 feet across. King George III is said to have walked through the huge tube. It was larger than any telescope that exists in Britain today.

The "amateur" astronomer

William Herschel was the greatest astronomer of his time. He was born in Hanover, Germany, in 1738, but made his home in England, where he built his own telescopes and used them to make great discoveries.

He started life as a musician, but spent his spare hours observing the sky from his garden. He taught himself to grind and polish the best and largest mirrors of the age, and he built large telescopes to contain them.

In 1781, from his home in Bath, he made his most famous discovery — the planet Uranus. But his most important observations were of the stars. He discovered hundreds of twin stars, known as **binary stars**, that orbit around each other. He also cataloged thousands of **star clusters** and nebulas — vast glowing clouds of gas out of which new stars form. By noting the numbers and the brightness of stars in different directions in the sky, he worked out that the Sun is just one star belonging to a vast "star city," which we now call the **Milky Way** Galaxy. His amazing industry traced the path for modern astronomers to follow.

Modern observatories are built on mountains far away from city lights, which would interfere with the view, in fair-weather regions of the Earth. The Cerro Tololo Inter-American Observatory at La Serena, Chile, is 7,872 feet above sea level, overlooking the Pacific Ocean.

The picture above shows the domes, which house large and small telescopes.

The main telescope at Cerro Tololo is shown on the right. It has a mirror 13 feet in diameter, which makes objects look a quarter of a million times brighter than when seen with the human eye. The mirror is hidden inside the bottom of the skeleton tube, but you can see the triangular flaps that close down to protect it. This is the fifth largest telescope in the world.

Telescopes today

The largest telescope in the world was completed in 1977. This is the 20-foot reflector on Mount Pastukhov, a mountain peak 6,800 feet high in the Soviet Union. Before that the famous 200-inch reflector at Mount Palomar in California (height 5,600 feet) was the world's largest.

The mounting or stand of a telescope is just as important as the tube and mirror. Since the Earth spins once a day, all objects in the sky seem to move around us once in this time. This means that a telescope has to be able to move also, to keep a star or planet in view. It is the mounting, the large horseshoe-shape shown in the picture above, that turns slowly, carrying the telescope with it.

Astronomers do not look through these huge telescopes directly. Instead, they use them to take photographs of the sky. These telescopes are really just giant cameras. Astronomers from all over the world will "book" time on a big telescope and spend perhaps a week at the observatory making careful observations.

15

Radio astronomy

Radio telescopes do not look anything like ordinary telescopes. This is because radio waves are invisible, and they cannot be reflected by a glass lens or a shiny mirror. The "mirror" used in a radio telescope is usually a bowl of metal or wire mesh. Some radio telescopes are nothing more than a collection of antennas spread over a field.

Radio telescopes cannot take photographs, but they can discover objects that cannot be seen with ordinary telescopes. For example, very cool stars send out powerful radio waves, but are almost too dim to be seen through a telescope. The spinning stars known as **pulsars** (see page 90) were discovered using radio telescopes, although once they were known to exist their "pulses" could be seen using ordinary telescopes.

Another great advantage of using radio telescopes is that they can pick up radio signals through clouds of **dust** in space that completely block out visible light. Because of this, radio astronomers have found out a great deal about the center of our Galaxy, which is hidden from view by these dust clouds. Radio telescopes can also see through the clouds in our own sky, and can listen to space by day as well as by night!

Some far distant galaxies also send out strong radio waves, even though they are only faintly seen in photographs. Therefore, radio telescopes are important for probing the limits of the universe.

Radio waves and light waves are both forms of energy. They are made up of minute "packets" of energy, which spread out in regular waves from an energy source. The type of light that we see has about 50,000 waves in every inch, but radio waves may be thousands of yards long.

Other kinds of energy waves also come from space. Some of them, such as gamma rays and X rays, are so powerful that they can kill living things. Fortunately, not all the waves reach the Earth's surface because our atmosphere blocks them out. Only satellites or rockets can pick up all the rays from space.

This radio telescope at Effelsberg, West Germany, has a bowl or "dish" 328 feet across. This collects the radio waves from space and focuses them onto a sensitive antenna, shown at the top of the four "legs." The result is not a picture but a hiss, like a badly tuned radio. A computer then sorts out the radio signal from the background "noise."

Radio telescopes are also used to receive signals from orbiting satellites and spacecrafts.

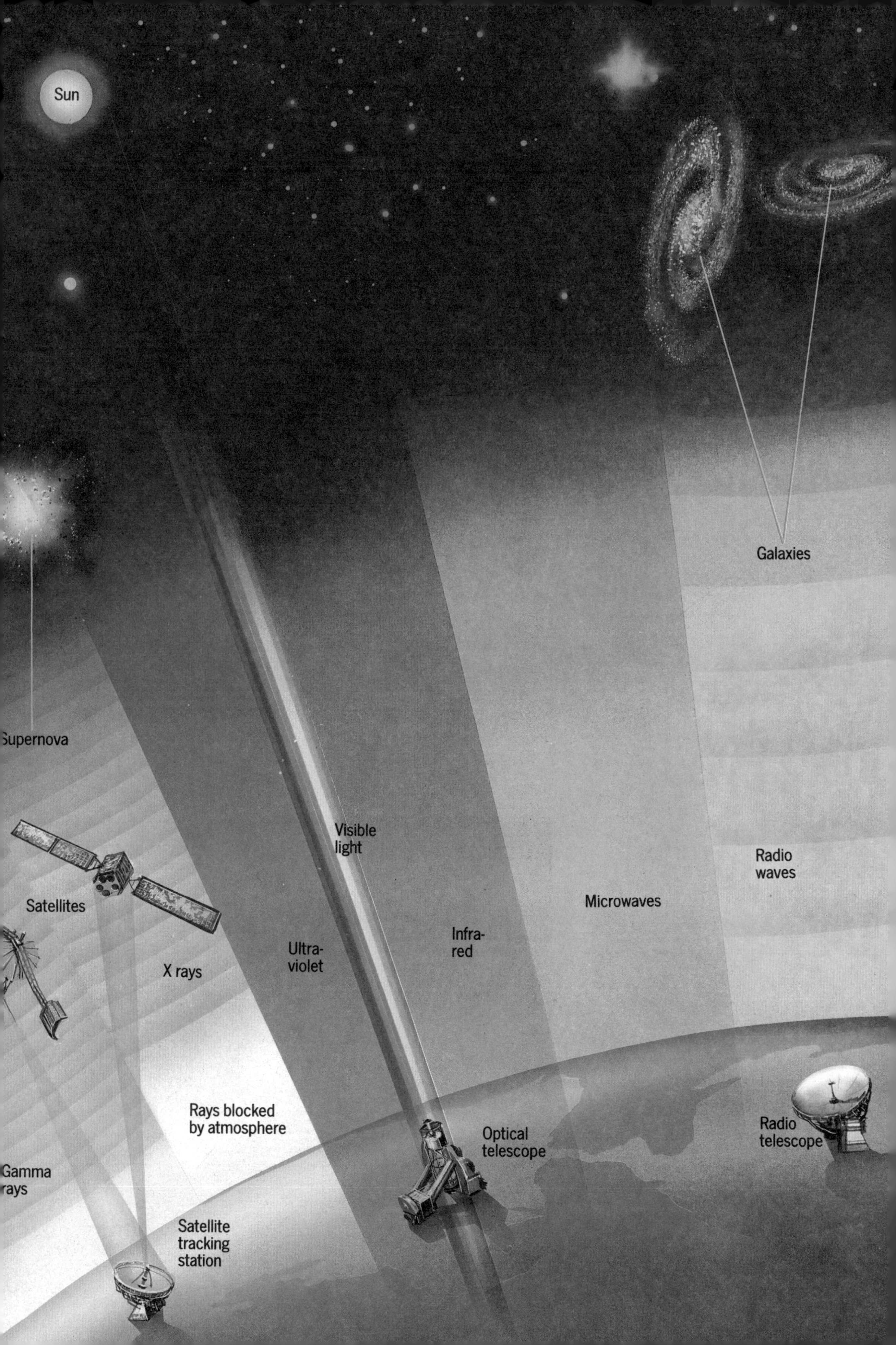

Sun

Galaxies

Supernova

Satellites

Visible
light

Radio
waves

Microwaves

X rays

Ultra-
violet

Infra-
red

Rays blocked
by atmosphere

Optical
telescope

Radio
telescope

Gamma
rays

Satellite
tracking
station

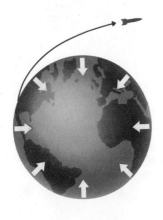

An orbiting satellite must be launched at just the right speed. Too slow, and it will fall back to Earth.

If it is launched too fast, it will escape from the pull of the Earth and fly off into space, never to return.

Launched at the correct speed, it will keep "falling" at the same rate as the Earth's surface curves away beneath it. This is known as "free fall." The Moon, in its much larger orbit, is in free fall around the Earth.

Out into space

Space travel had been a fantastic dream for so long that the world was taken completely by surprise when the Soviet Union launched the first artificial satellite Sputnik 1 on October 4, 1957. Two years later, a Soviet rocket hit the Moon, and in 1961 a Russian became the first man in space. At the same time, the United States announced its plans to send men to the Moon by the end of the decade, and this feat was achieved in 1969.

Nowadays, space travel is taken so much for granted that successful satellite or space-probe launches do not attract much attention. It took the explosion of the *Challenger* Space Shuttle in January 1986 to remind the public that risks are still involved, and that to be an astronaut you must be brave as well as fit.

For astronomers, putting telescopes and instruments into space has two big advantages. First, equipment launched in a satellite can pick up all the different kinds of energy waves sent out by an object — not just those that pass through our **atmosphere.** Second, space probes can get close-up views of the other planets in our solar system, and may even land on their surfaces.

The accuracy with which spacecrafts can be guided by remote control toward distant planets is amazing, but this would be useless without good communications to send the information back to Earth. It is incredible to think that the detailed pictures sent back by the Voyager 2 probe from the planet Uranus in 1986 were transmitted using less energy than a car headlight bulb!

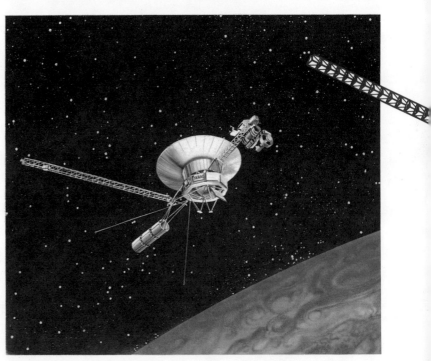

The first satellite in space — Sputnik 1.

Spaceman Yuri Gagarin.

SOME "FIRSTS" IN SPACE EXPLORATION

1957 The U.S.S.R. launches the satellite Sputnik 1.
1958 The U.S.A. launches Explorer 1.
1959 Rockets from the U.S.S.R. reach the Moon.
1961 The Russian Yuri Gagarin orbits the Earth.
1962 Mariner 2 (U.S.A.) flies past Venus.
1965 Mariner 4 (U.S.A.) flies past Mars.
1966 Venera 3 (U.S.S.R.) lands on Venus.
1969 The manned Apollo 11 (U.S.A.) lands on the Moon.
1973 Pioneer 10 (U.S.A.) flies past Jupiter.
1976 Two Viking spacecrafts (U.S.A.) land on Mars.
1979 Pioneer 11 flies past Saturn.
1981 The first Space Shuttle (U.S.A.) is launched.
1986 Voyager 2 (U.S.A.) flies past Uranus, and probes take close-up pictures of Halley's comet.

The Apollo 11 rocket launch.

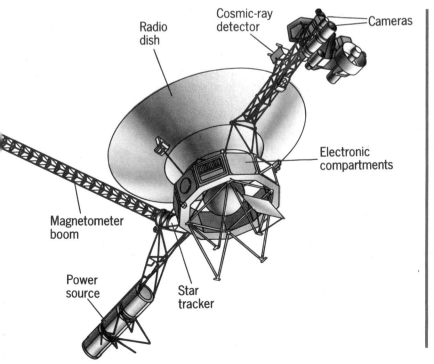

Radio dish

Cosmic-ray detector

Cameras

Electronic compartments

Magnetometer boom

Power source

Star tracker

The Voyager 2 probe, shown on the left and on the opposite page, was launched in 1977 from Cape Canaveral, in Florida. It is the most successful planetary traveler of all time. It has sent back amazing close-up pictures of the planets Jupiter, Saturn, and Uranus, as well as views of their moons. It has also discovered more moons for all these planets. It is now due to reach Neptune in 1989, after which it will fly off on an eternal journey among the stars.

2. The Solar System

A family of planets

We live on a small planet, the Earth, orbiting an average star, the Sun. If you imagine the Sun to be the size of an orange, a scale model showing all the nine planets in the solar system would fit into a large field. But to find the next nearest star after the Sun, you would have to look for another orange about 1,240 miles away.

This means that the Sun and its planets are really a very lonely group in the immensity of space, so it is natural to look upon the planets as members of a "family." But it is a strange family in some ways — all the planets were probably born at the same time, but there are big differences between them.

The Sun shines, the planets do not. Therefore we only see the planets because of the sunlight shining on them. From the Earth, the planets look just like stars in the night sky, but as they orbit the Sun they change their positions in the night sky compared with the patterns of the far-off stars.

The nearer a planet is to the Sun, the shorter its "year" — the time it takes to orbit the Sun once. Innermost Mercury has a year of only 88 Earth days, while outermost Pluto's is two and a half Earth centuries.

As well as the nine planets, most of which have natural satellites or **moons** of their own, there are also much smaller solid bodies known as minor planets or **asteroids**. There are also countless pieces of solid matter, most smaller than a marble but some as large as a football. These are known as meteoroids. Finally there are the comets, some of which take many thousands of years to orbit the Sun once.

This view of the Sun and planets shows how small the Earth is compared with the four "giant planets." But even the giants are tiny compared with the Sun.

Below: The nine planets of the solar system are:
1. Mercury
2. Venus
3. Earth
4. Mars
5. Jupiter
6. Saturn
7. Uranus
8. Neptune
9. Pluto

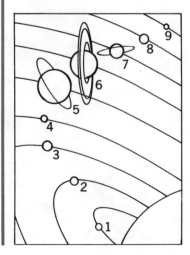

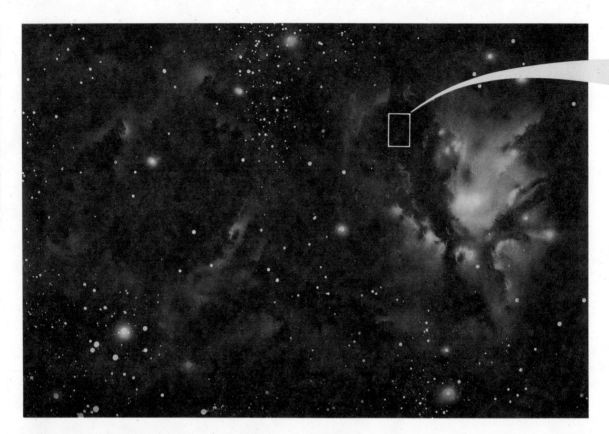

The birth of the stars

We think the Sun was born about four and a half billion years ago. Spread between the stars there are huge dark clouds of powder-sized solid particles and hydrogen gas. These are known as nebulas. A sudden disturbance, such as the blast from an exploding star — a **supernova** — can start a ripple passing through a nebula. The result is that the nebula starts to break up into a group of smaller clouds, and these clouds shrink inward and start to spin. A young star is formed at the center of each cloud, and it spins once in just a few hours.

If this theory is true, then the Sun must have been born with other stars, in a group or cluster. But over the billions of years since they formed, these stars have drifted apart. We have no idea now where the other members of the Sun's original family of stars have wandered to.

A shrinking cloud

When you pump up a bicycle tire, the pump begins to feel hot at the point where the air is being forced through the narrow nozzle. This is because the air is being squeezed or "compressed" into a smaller space. The same thing happened to the cloud from which our Sun was formed. As the particles at the center became crowded together they grew hot. Eventually, a cloud a thousand times

Dark patches seen among the stars are known as nebulas. Because they are so far away they look small, but each nebula is millions of times bigger than the solar system, and contains enough gas and dust to make hundreds of stars.

New stars are being formed all the time. When old stars grow dim and cold, a lot of the material in them is thrown out into space, and later on may be "recycled," through nebulas, into new stars.

Since the Sun is only about a quarter as old as the universe, our solar system may have been formed from older stars.

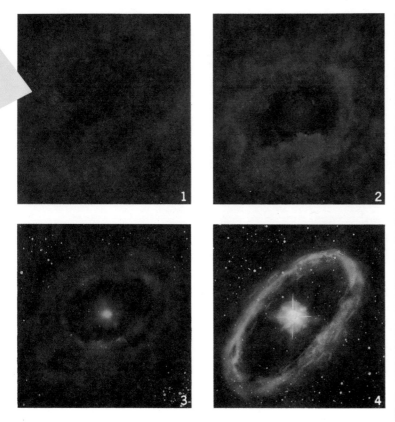

The early stages of the formation of the solar system may have looked like this.

1. A part of a nebula begins to collapse into a black mass of hydrogen gas and small solid particles of "dust."

2. As the center becomes hot, because of the increasing pressure, it starts to glow dim and red.

3. The hot center now starts to shine more brightly because nuclear reactions have begun and are giving out huge amounts of heat — it is a recognizable star, surrounded by a ring of material reflecting its light.

4. As the Sun comes up to full power, the ring starts to condense into more solid pieces.

bigger than the solar system shrank down to the size of the Sun, spinning faster and faster as it did so, surrounded by a huge halo of gas and dust particles.

During this shrinking, the center of the cloud became as hot as an electric heater, then as hot as a steel furnace, and finally reached the fantastic temperature of several million degrees. At this point, the center of the Sun turned into a nuclear bomb. It did not blow up, because the outer layers were like the lid on a pressure cooker, but the tremendous heat made the temperature rise to about 27 million degrees, which is the temperature inside the Sun now.

But something also happened to the halo of spare material around the young Sun. Instead of just drifting off into space, or falling inward onto the Sun's surface, it formed a ring rather like a doughnut, whirling around the Sun at high speed. This was the material that would form our Sun's planets, including the Earth.

Astronomers have not yet been able to see any planets around other stars, but it seems likely that many stars were born with planets, or planet-making materials, orbiting around them. If so, planets are probably very common throughout the universe and, even more importantly, other life-forms apart from our own may be very common as well.

The birth of the planets

The ring or doughnut circling the young Sun contained gas (mostly hydrogen, but also other common gases such as nitrogen) and tiny specks of solid material such as carbon and iron. In fact, all the **elements** — the basic ingredients that are found today on the Earth and in the other planets — were there, all mixed up together.

The planets formed because the small pieces of solid matter in the ring collided to make larger and larger pieces or "bodies." These collisions were so violent that the bodies became red-hot. If you could heat a mixture of elements in a fireproof container until they melted, you would notice that the heavier ones sink below the lighter ones. Iron and other metals are heavier than rock, for example. This is why the planets have central "cores" made of iron, nickel, and other metals, with a layer of rock or gas above.

You might wonder why the ring broke up into a system of planets, instead of another star or even a set of stars. Why isn't the Earth, or Jupiter, a star instead of a planet? The reason is that these bodies did not become large enough, and therefore hot enough, to start the nuclear reactions that make the stars shine (see page 38).

Not even giant Jupiter was quite large enough to turn into a star. If it had, there would have been two suns in our sky! But it is interesting that the same ingredients can make a star or a planet — it simply depends upon how much material is available.

The distant star Vega is thought to have a doughnut-like ring of gas and dust swirling around it. If it has, it may be forming its own solar system of planets.

This may have been how our own solar system looked before the planets were formed.

HOW THE PLANETS FORMED

The planets may have formed out of the "doughnut" rather like this.

1. To begin with, the doughnut was a spinning ring of gas and dust.

2. The solid particles began to strike each other and stick together, forming larger bodies. At first, these were mostly carbon and ice.

3. These particles rapidly grew to planetary size. As they grew larger they began to "pull" against each other, which meant that if they passed too close to each other, they were pulled into a different orbit. Some of the very small carbon-ice bodies were pulled so violently by the larger ones that they were thrown right out toward the stars, while others found themselves pulled into very long orbits that carried them far beyond the planets and back again very near to the Sun. These are the comets (see page 36).

4. Eventually there were just a few large bodies going around the Sun in orbits that did not meet each other, and so there were no more collisions or near misses — the nine major planets were formed.

5. With the passage of billions of years the planets continued to pull against each other, until their orbits have become almost level.

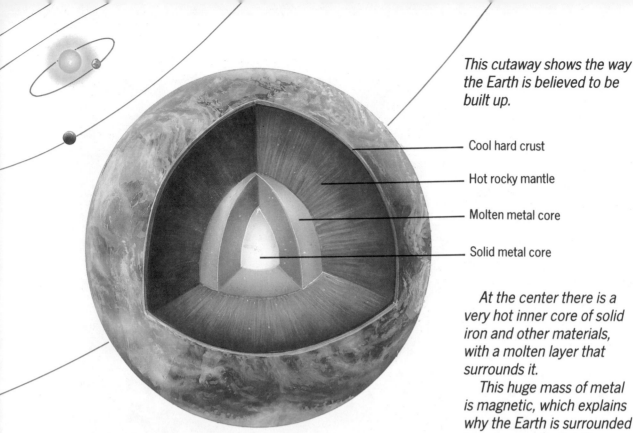

This cutaway shows the way the Earth is believed to be built up.

Cool hard crust
Hot rocky mantle
Molten metal core
Solid metal core

At the center there is a very hot inner core of solid iron and other materials, with a molten layer that surrounds it.

This huge mass of metal is magnetic, which explains why the Earth is surrounded by a "magnetic field" — an area of magnetism that spreads outward from the core and into space (see page 45). Around the core is the mantle, which is the thickest layer of the Earth, and on top of the mantle is a surface skin of much cooler, solid rock, the crust.

Since large bodies cool more slowly than small ones, the inside of the Earth has remained much hotter since it was formed than the inside of Mercury or Mars. Eventually, our planet will completely cool down and become solid.

The inner planets

The four planets nearest the Sun form a special family of their own. They are much smaller than the four distant giant planets, and they are made up differently, being rocky globes instead of gas and ice.

When they formed, the inner planets must have grown so hot that they became liquid, or molten. The metallic particles, such as iron and nickel, were the heaviest part of the mixture and sank down toward the center, forming the core. This left the particles of rock to form a thick layer above the core. Then the surface of the rocky layer cooled to form a skin or "crust." Other small objects still orbiting the Sun plunged into the crust, leaving their marks as **craters**.

The smallest of these planets, innermost Mercury, cooled the fastest, and these ancient craters are still visible. It is the only inner planet with no atmosphere at all, and its craters prove that nothing much has changed there for perhaps 4 billion years. The larger planets Venus and the Earth cooled more slowly, and on the Earth molten rock still floods out through the crust in volcanic eruptions. The fourth planet, Mars, is a strange mixture of ancient craters and much newer volcanic mountains.

There are other differences between the inner planets beside these. The atmosphere of Venus is thicker than water and its surface is hotter than any other planet in the

solar system. Active volcanoes may still be erupting here and tremors could still shake its surface, as on the Earth. Mars has only a thin atmosphere (one hundred times thinner than our own), but even this has made a big difference to the surface, raising huge dust-storms that have gradually worn away many of the old craters. Its volcanoes all seem to be dead now.

The Earth is the only planet that has huge areas of water on its surface. It is at just the right distance from the Sun for water to be liquid instead of frozen or steam. This is one reason why life has developed here. Compared with its neighbor worlds, the Earth is a colorful and exotic place.

The closest place to the Sun is Mercury's surface, shown above. With its mountains and craters it looks like our Moon. The huge Sun blazes down on an airless world.

The most distant of the inner planets is shown below. White hoar frost sparkles on the barren ground of Mars long before the Sun goes down in the pink sky.

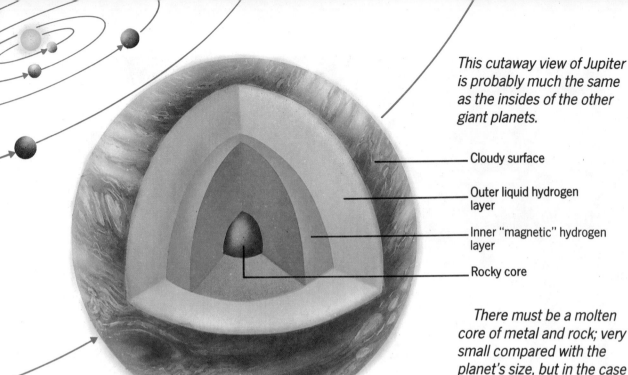

This cutaway view of Jupiter is probably much the same as the insides of the other giant planets.

- Cloudy surface
- Outer liquid hydrogen layer
- Inner "magnetic" hydrogen layer
- Rocky core

There must be a molten core of metal and rock; very small compared with the planet's size, but in the case of Jupiter and Saturn probably larger than the Earth. This is where the iron, nickel, and other metals, which are invisible in the clouds covering the surface, must be found.

The rest of the planet is made of hydrogen, with a thin covering of hydrogen mixed with other frozen substances in the form of swirling icy clouds.

The outer planets

The enormous, frozen globes of the giant outer planets make even chilly Mars seem close to the Sun's welcoming warmth. They are different in every way from the inner planets — in size, makeup, temperature, and length of day. But while the inner planets have big differences among themselves, what we know of the giant planets — Jupiter, Saturn, Uranus, and Neptune — suggests that they are fairly similar.

These planets are not rocky — in fact, they are mostly made of hydrogen gas. On the Earth, hydrogen is such a light gas that it was once used to make balloons and airships fly, but on the outer planets it forms icy clouds and liquids. Other elements, such as nitrogen and carbon, are also found in the outer planets. These have mixed with the hydrogen to form the dark or colored bands that are especially obvious on Jupiter.

The giant planets spin faster than the inner planets. This has made them bulge out at the equator, proving that they are made of liquid, not solid rock.

Another feature of the giant planets is the **rings** circling at least three of them. The bright rings of Saturn are the only ones that can be seen through a telescope, but Jupiter and Uranus also have faint rings, as discovered by space probes. These rings may be made from particles trapped by the planets' **gravity** soon after they formed, before the rings could gather into larger bodies.

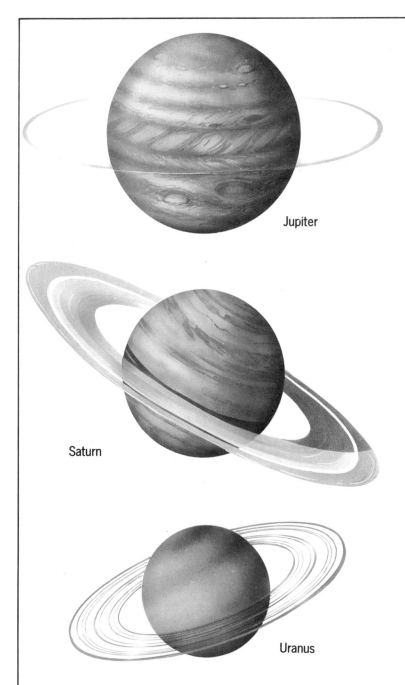

Jupiter

Saturn

Uranus

RINGED PLANETS

The giant planets Jupiter, Saturn, and Uranus all have thin bands or "rings" spinning around them. These rings are made up of countless rocky or icy fragments less than a yard across.

Jupiter's ring, the most recently discovered, is extremely narrow and dim — it cannot be seen properly except in photographs taken in space. It also has a much larger, even fainter ring of sulfur particles.

Saturn's bright rings are one of the showpieces of the sky. They contain thousands of narrow ringlets, one inside the other.

The ring system of Uranus consists of 13 narrow ringlets spaced wide apart. It is possible that the fourth giant planet, Neptune, also has a dim ring system. These ring systems may have been formed from stray particles, or possibly from one or more very small satellites that broke up.

It is also possible that the rings were formed when a solid body was captured by the planets' gravity. Being so close, the gravitational force strained and broke the body apart, and the pieces collided with each other, wearing themselves down into the small fragments that now form the rings.

The ninth planet, Pluto, is unlike all the other planets. It is usually known as the "outermost" planet. At the present time, however, Pluto is the eighth planet as it is currently closer to the Sun than Neptune. Distant Pluto is a mysterious world of its own; it is the smallest planet in the solar system, and is probably solid ice.

The satellites

Altogether, 64 satellites or moons have been discovered orbiting the planets in the solar system — only Mercury and Venus do not appear to have any. Close-up photographs of satellites taken by space probes (especially the amazing Voyager 2) show a strange variety of surfaces — icy, rocky, or covered with brightly colored chemicals. But almost all of them are marked by craters as well.

This shows that there were once many other rocky bodies orbiting the Sun. Most of these have now been destroyed after colliding with the planets or their moons, leaving only a crater to mark their existence. Those that are left now belong to the realm of the minor planets or asteroids that orbit beyond the distance of Mars, but closer than Jupiter.

The giant planets have many satellites. A total of 24 have been found orbiting Saturn. Most satellites are small, less than 70 miles across. They were probably "captured" by the planets' gravity when they were revolving around the Sun in their own orbits, back in the early days of the solar system. But there are also much larger satellites. The picture on this page shows the sizes of the four largest moons of Jupiter, compared with our own Moon. It is likely that these satellites, like our Moon, formed separately, at the same time as the planets, from the rings or clouds of material in orbit around each planet — like miniature solar systems.

Earth's Moon

Io

Europa

Ganymede

Callisto

Three of Jupiter's four largest satellites are bigger than our Moon, and Ganymede is even larger than the planet Mercury. The diagram shows their orbits around Jupiter.

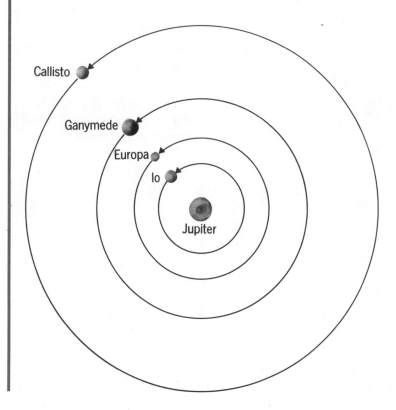

Callisto

Ganymede

Europa

Io

Jupiter

If astronauts ever venture out as far as the realm of the giant planets, they will choose a satellite as a landing place. A spacecraft would be sucked down to destruction if it headed for the planet itself. This view might be seen by travelers heading for one of Jupiter's satellites.

Most satellites appear to be dead and unchanging, like our Moon. But one moon, Jupiter's Io, is covered with patches of sulfur and has erupting volcanoes spouting material out into space. Another unusual moon, Saturn's Titan, has an atmosphere of nitrogen gas.

Even tiny remote Pluto, which is smaller than Jupiter's moons Ganymede and Callisto, has its own satellite, Charon, half as big as itself. Some astronomers think of Pluto and Charon as a "double planet." Undoubtedly there are many more tiny satellites belonging to the outer planets still waiting to be discovered. Voyager 2 may find some other moons orbiting Neptune.

The surface of Mimas, one of the moons of Saturn, is proof of the violent collisions that must have occurred when there were many whirling pieces of rock in the solar system. If the huge crater that you can see on the right had been much bigger, Mimas would have broken up completely.

The minor planets

If you look at a map of the solar system, you will see a very large "gap" between the orbits of Mars and Jupiter, as though there should be another planet there. This realization led to a hunt, in the late 18th century, for the "missing planet," and not one but many minor planets or asteroids were discovered.

Most of the three thousand or so asteroids that have been found orbit the Sun in a "belt" at about the distance where the missing planet should be, but some minor planets also pass very close to the Sun, or out beyond the realm of Saturn.

Pieces of planet

The largest asteroid, Ceres, is about 600 miles across. But if all the asteroids, and others suspected to exist but not yet identified, were lumped together they would still not make up a body as big as the Moon. This means it is very unlikely that the minor planets were formed by two large planets colliding and breaking up. What is much more likely is that the powerful gravity of Jupiter, in the next orbit outward from the Sun, stopped a large planet forming in the first place, leaving some of the "ingredients" behind.

We have one important clue to the origin of the minor planets. Some seem to be made of very dark rock, while others are made of lighter rock, and a few are as shiny as metal. The metal particles in the Sun's original nebula would not come naturally together in this way — they must have been heated and melted. Therefore it is likely

This diagram shows the main belt of minor planets, as well as a few that have more unusual orbits. There are certain to be many other minor planets with strange orbits, but discovering them is mainly a matter of luck, because they are so small and faint.

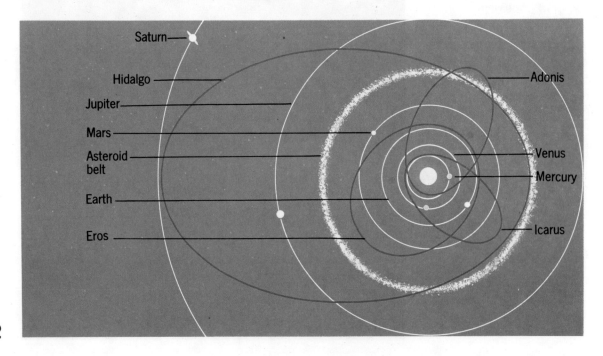

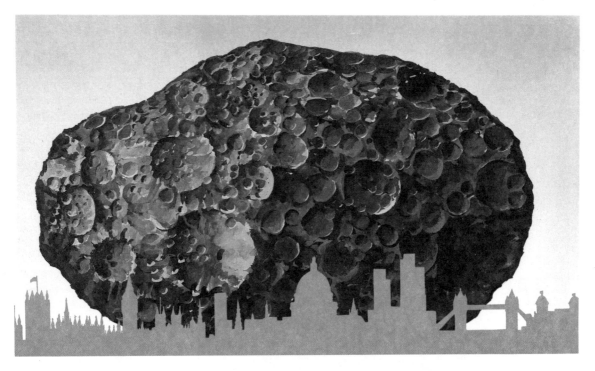

A very small asteroid compared in size with part of London. There are probably thousands of bodies as small as this in the solar system.

A tiny asteroid containing precious metals is towed into orbit around the Earth, where it will be mined.

that at least one very small rocky planet, with an iron core, did begin to form before it was broken up again.

Even a small asteroid is as large as a city, and if one struck the Earth it would leave a crater a hundred times as large as itself and could devastate a whole country. However, since careful observations began, no asteroid has been known to approach our planet within a million miles.

The minor planets could become very important to us in the future. If we could find a way to mine them they may contain valuable metals and minerals that are in short supply on the Earth.

High above the Earth, a meteoroid dashes into the atmosphere. At a height of about 50 miles above the Earth there is enough air to cause a glow; most meteors have burned up at about 20 miles. In the photograph below, a camera with its shutter left open has recorded a number of streaks during a meteor shower.

Shooting stars

Wait for a clear, moonless night, and settle yourself down comfortably in a place with a good view of the stars. Make sure your eyes are shielded from dazzling artificial lights, and you will probably see at least three or four "shooting stars" or **meteors** within about half an hour. Meteors are trails of glowing superheated air, caused by tiny marble-sized particles, known as meteoroids, rushing into the atmosphere at speeds of up to 30 miles a second. The atmosphere slows down the meteoroid and it ends its brief glory as fine grains of meteoric dust, which float unnoticed down to the ground.

Meteoroids orbit the Sun in the millions. Many move in large groups or swarms. They almost certainly began life as comets, which gradually scatter their own waste particles into space. After the comet itself has faded away, the particles remain, traveling along the comet's old orbit. When the Earth passes through one of these orbits, the number of meteors that can be seen increases for a time. This is a meteor shower.

Meteor showers can be seen at certain dates every year. One of the best is seen around August 12, when dozens of meteors may flash into view every hour. These meteors are known as the Perseids, because they appear to come from a point in the sky that lies in the star group or **constellation** known as Perseus.

A meteoroid swarm may be spread out along a huge orbit around the Sun, so that a single particle takes years to go around once. If the Earth passes through the swarm a meteor shower will be seen.

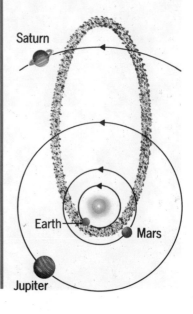

Hundreds of larger meteoroids, known as meteorites, hit the Earth every day, but very few are found. Some, however, cannot be missed. This house in Connecticut had a meteorite weighing almost 7 pounds crash through its roof in November 1982. During its fall, the streak of light lit up the whole sky.

Meteor Crater in Arizona is the best example of an impact crater in the whole world. It is over 3,300 feet across and 650 feet deep, and the collision probably took place about 25,000 years ago.

The Earth must once have been covered with craters much larger than this, but they have been worn down by weather and surface movements.

Meteorites

If a meteoroid is larger than a pebble, there is a good chance that it will not burn up in the atmosphere, and will hit the ground. This is a **meteorite**. At present, meteorites are the only chance we have to examine material from space. There are two main kinds — stony and metallic. The stony ones are much more common, but are harder to find on the ground because they look rather like any other dark stone. The metallic ones are mostly made of iron, and could come from the core of a small planet broken up by collisions.

The largest known meteorite weighs about 60 tons. It is iron, and lies where it fell in Namibia, in southwest Africa. A very large meteorite, or possibly the core or "nucleus" of a small comet, struck marshy ground in Siberia in 1908. The explosion was heard thousands of miles away. In 1976 a meteorite weighing almost 2 tons landed in China.

Above: The nucleus of Halley's comet was discovered to be a peanut-shaped mixture of rock, dust, and ice more than a mile long. The Sun's heat turned the ice into gas, and dust trapped in the ice was released. Each return to the Sun leaves the nucleus with a smaller store of ice and dust, and eventually Halley's comet will "die."

This ancient drawing shows Halley's comet as seen over Jerusalem in A.D. 66.

Wanderers in space

Comets were once thought to foretell the coming of evil events, since they appeared so unexpectedly and dramatically. In fact, they orbit the Sun as obediently as the planets. The difference is that most comets have large, long orbits that carry them from near the Sun to beyond the giant planets, and even some way toward the nearest stars. They may take thousands of years to complete one orbit of the Sun, and so their reappearance in the sky can come as a complete surprise, since they have never been seen before in living memory.

Some comets have smaller orbits and pass near the Sun every few years. Halley's comet returned in the winter of 1985–86 after its previous visit in 1910. One of the brightest comets was Comet West, which appeared in 1976 and could be faintly seen in full daylight.

A comet's tail

The solid part, the nucleus of a comet, is very small — just about a mile across. What makes it shine is sunlight reflected by the huge halo of gas and dust, which is given off by the nucleus as it warms up near the Sun. If enough material is poured out, the comet may show a long glowing "tail" sweeping back through space. A comet's tail can be tens of millions of miles long, but a portion the size of the whole Earth would have only a few pounds of solid matter in it.

The nucleus of a comet is believed to be made of the crumbly, icy material that was formed when the solar nebula first began to shape itself into the planets. These small fragments did not become compressed together into solid planets, but kept on orbiting the Sun alone.

There may be millions of comets held weakly by the Sun's gravitational pull, passing far beyond the orbit of Pluto. Every few years, one of them begins the centuries-long journey inward toward the Sun's light and heat, and for a few nights people gaze in amazement at a glowing sword of light shining in the night sky.

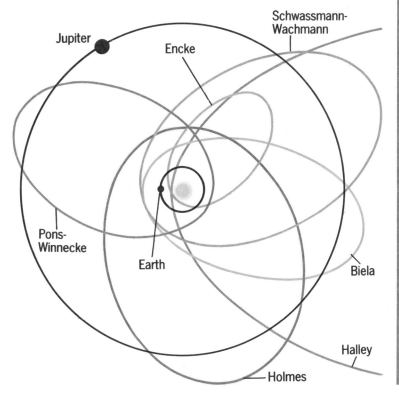

Comets are usually named after the person or people who discovered them. This diagram shows the orbits of some comets that return regularly to the Sun every few years. Part of the much bigger orbit of Halley's comet is also shown. Encke's comet has the smallest orbit, and it passes close to the Sun every three years and four months, although it cannot be seen without a telescope.

Several of the comets shown above are farthest from the Sun at about the same distance as the giant planet Jupiter. This has happened because the powerful gravitational pull of giant Jupiter has "trapped" them. If a comet passed too close to Jupiter it would find itself pulled into a completely new orbit, or even flung out of the solar system.

FAMOUS COMETS

Name	Orbital Period	First Seen
Encke's Comet	3.3 years	1786
Pons-Winnecke Comet	6.0 years	1819
Biela's Comet	6.7 years	1806
Holmes's Comet	6.85 years	1892
Schwassmann-Wachmann Comet	16.2 years	1925
Halley's Comet	76 years	240 B.C.
Ikeya-Seki Comet	880 years	1965
Donati's Comet	2040 years	1858
Humason's Comet	2900 years	1961
Arend-Roland Comet	10,000 years	1957
Kohoutek's Comet	75,000 years	1975

3. The Sun, Our Star

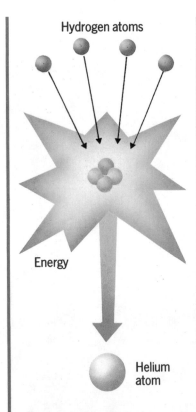

Hydrogen atoms

Energy

Helium atom

Four hydrogen atoms contain slightly more material than one helium atom. When the helium atom is formed, the extra material is destroyed in a flash of energy or heat. Every second, the Sun turns about four million tons of hydrogen material into energy in this way.

How the Sun shines

The Sun looks as if it is on fire, but it is not "burning" in the way that fire burns. Its surface shines brightly simply because it is very hot — about 11,000 degrees, which is far hotter than white-hot steel.

The source of this heat lies near the center of the Sun. This is its "atomic powerhouse," where the temperature of the hydrogen gas making up our star is thought to be about 27 million degrees. At this temperature, the particles in the invisibly small **atoms** that make up the hydrogen break apart and come together again in a different way, forming atoms of another gas called helium. This is known as an "atomic reaction," and when it takes place a flash of energy is given out. Countless billions of flashes of energy every second keep the center of the Sun hot.

This energy takes a long time to reach the Sun's surface. In fact, the heat coming from the surface of the Sun today was created by atomic reactions that happened a million years ago! Some astronomers have wondered if the Sun's center is producing less energy now than it once was. If this is so, only far future generations will notice the surface cooling down.

The layers of the Sun

Once the hydrogen deep inside the Sun has changed to helium, it sinks into the brilliant core of helium that has built up at the very center of our star. Outside this is a layer of hydrogen heated by the core shining on it. During the next few billion years, some of this hydrogen will also be turned into helium. Farther up in the Sun, where the

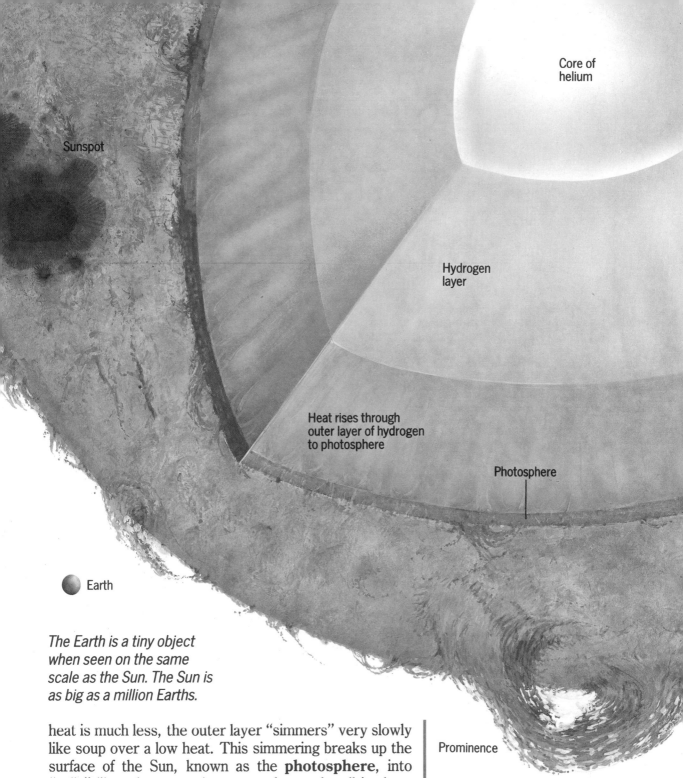

Core of helium

Hydrogen layer

Heat rises through outer layer of hydrogen to photosphere

Photosphere

Sunspot

Earth

The Earth is a tiny object when seen on the same scale as the Sun. The Sun is as big as a million Earths.

Prominence

heat is much less, the outer layer "simmers" very slowly like soup over a low heat. This simmering breaks up the surface of the Sun, known as the **photosphere**, into "cells" like a honeycomb, except that each cell is about 600 miles across.

Here and there on the photosphere, cooler patches look dark compared with the rest of the shining surface. These are the **sunspots**.

How long can the Sun keep shining before it uses up all its hydrogen and has no more energy to give out? Astronomers have worked out that the Sun has so far used up much less than half of its supply of hydrogen. On pages 46 and 47 we look at what may happen in the distant future, when our star runs into a "fuel crisis."

To us the Sun is too bright to look at, and it is foolish and dangerous to try. But the surface is quite dim and cool compared with the center. If this was opened up and we could see the core, the Earth would be turned to a cinder in minutes.

39

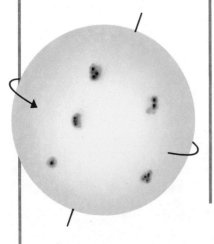

The Sun spins around once in 27 days.

As the Sun turns from day to day the sunspots seem to move with it, traveling across the Sun's face.

The Sun's surface

The Sun was once thought to be a perfect shining ball. But as soon as telescopes were invented, astronomers were able to see that it is continually changing. Dark spots appear and disappear, and huge flares of gas leap from its surface.

Sunspots

Sunspots look dark because they are cooler than the rest of the Sun's surface — a cool surface gives out less light than a bright one. The center or "umbra" of a sunspot has a temperature of about 7,000 degrees, and the outer part or "penumbra" is about 9,000 degrees, compared with the 11,000-degrees of the rest of the surface.

A sunspot as large as the Earth is considered very small indeed. Some have spread over an area several times larger. These large spots are usually made up of at least two main spots, with other smaller ones nearby. They may last for several weeks before fading.

Sunspots appear most frequently every 11 years or so. At these "maximum" times a dozen different spot groups may be visible at the same time. At "minimum" activity, however, the Sun's disk may not show a single spot. The next maximum phase is due in the early 1990s. No one knows why this 11-year cycle happens.

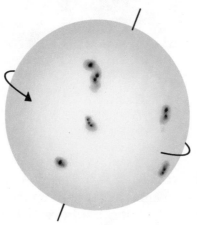

During their journey some spots fade and others appear. They are changing all the time.

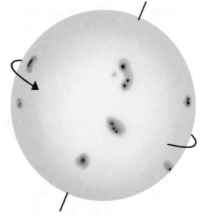

The spinning Sun

The Sun spins around once in 27 days. If you could study it every day, you would see the sunspot groups appearing to move steadily across its face, taking two weeks to pass from one edge to the other. During this time, some groups will also fade out and others will be formed. A sunspot can grow very quickly, reaching the size of the Earth in a matter of hours. The largest sunspot group ever seen, in 1947, was about 150,000 miles long — 20 times the Earth's diameter.

STUDYING THE SUN

Every year, people are partially blinded because they look at the Sun either with the naked eye or through binoculars. It is foolish to take this risk when there is a completely safe way of studying it.

The safe way is to use the "projection" method. Position a piece of white card about a foot behind the eyepieces of a pair of binoculars, and move the binoculars around until an image (or rather two images) of the Sun appear on the paper. You will have to move the eyepieces a little farther out from their normal viewing position to get a really sharp image.

Shield the card from direct sunlight by using a second piece of card to cast a shadow. You should be able to see any sunspot groups quite easily, but you must mount the binoculars firmly on a stand, so that the image is steady. Either use a proper mounting, or make your own setup like the one shown here. Cover one of the binocular lenses to avoid an overlapping image.

WARNING:
Some stores sell "Sun filters" to allow you to look through a telescope, or binoculars, at the Sun. Do not use them — there is a terrible risk of blinding yourself if you make a mistake. Instead, use this simple setup to observe sunspots safely, using binoculars.

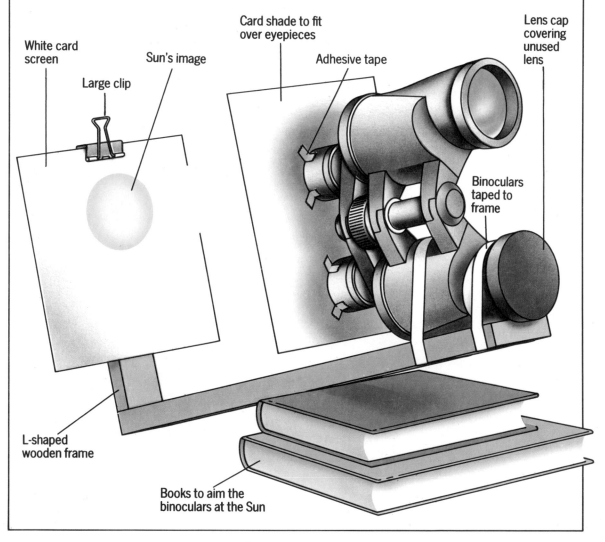

White card screen

Large clip

Sun's image

Card shade to fit over eyepieces

Adhesive tape

Lens cap covering unused lens

Binoculars taped to frame

L-shaped wooden frame

Books to aim the binoculars at the Sun

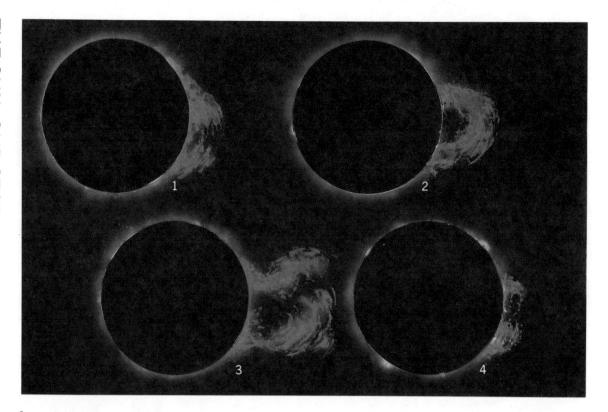

The flaring prominences

Photographs of the Sun show it looking like a round disk with a sharp edge. But this disk is only the brightly shining surface. Above the surface, plumes of glowing hydrogen known as **prominences** spout into space.

Prominences are of different kinds. There are the "quiet" kind, which do not show much change for weeks at a time. Some of these look like a branching tree. There are others that last for only a few days, rising from the surface to form colossal arches, as high as ten Earths piled on top of each other, before fading away. There are also very violent "explosive" prominences, which shoot off the Sun's surface at speeds as great as 600 miles per second. These fly off into space and never return, since the Sun's gravity is not powerful enough to pull them back again.

The only time these prominences can be seen from the Earth is during a total **eclipse** of the Sun. When an eclipse happens, the brilliant face of the Sun is blocked from our view by the Moon, and any prominences spouting from the edge of the Sun can be seen as pinkish-red shapes around the black circle of the Moon. They are pink because this is the color of hydrogen gas when it is very hot.

Special telescopes on the Earth, and other instruments carried into space by satellites, can also photograph prominences at other times, so that astronomers can study them continuously for days on end, seeing how they develop and then fade away.

This series of views shows how an explosive prominence bursts up from the edge of the Sun over a period of two days. A thin bright layer of glowing hydrogen gas, the "chromosphere," can be seen around the edge of the hidden Sun.

A "quiet" arched prominence, with a dot representing the size of the Earth on the same scale.

The corona

The Sun is surrounded by a huge, faintly glowing halo called the **corona,** which stretches for millions of miles out into space. It shines in the same way that fog particles glow around a streetlight. The difference is that the particles in the corona are mainly **electrons** — minute pieces of atoms — and not foggy waterdrops. The corona is almost as thin as empty space, and far thinner than a comet's tail, for example. It can only be seen because it is so huge.

The corona, like the prominences, can only be seen during a total solar eclipse. Then, for a short and wonderful time, it appears like a pale flower around the black Moon. The particles that form the corona are in fact rushing away from the Sun, being replaced by other particles rising from the surface. They spread out invisibly through the solar system, causing what is known as the **solar wind**. In fact, they carry on out past the planets into deep space, where they merge with the particles flowing outward from other stars. This means that our own planet is inside the Sun's corona, too.

The delicate glow of the Sun's corona can be seen when the bright light from its surface is hidden from view by the Moon. If you are lucky enough to see a total eclipse of the Sun you may see the corona extending into space for two or three times as far as shown here.

Notice how the corona has short "plumes" at the top and bottom points on the Sun's edge. This is where the Sun's strong magnetic force has "brushed" it into strands.

If you sprinkle iron filings on a sheet of paper, with a magnet underneath the paper, the filings form themselves into the same sort of lines. The Sun is like a huge magnet.

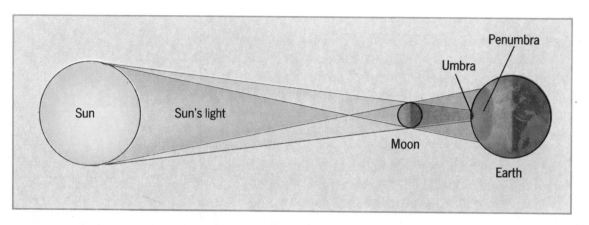

Penumbra
Umbra
Sun
Sun's light
Moon
Earth

Seen from the Earth

By a strange coincidence, the Sun and the Moon seem almost exactly the same size in our sky. If the Moon passes in front of the Sun during its monthly journey around the Earth, it can block out the brilliant disk from view. This is called a total eclipse of the Sun.

The Moon's distance from us changes slightly as it goes around the Earth, and if it is too far away when an eclipse occurs it does not appear large enough to cover the Sun completely. This is called an "annular eclipse."

Early astronomers puzzled over these events. They discovered that if an eclipse happens, there is certain to be another one exactly 18 years 10 days and 6 hours afterward. Some people have even suggested that ancient stone circles like Stonehenge, in England, were used to calculate the dates of future eclipses of the Sun and the Moon.

A total eclipse of the Sun can only be seen from a very small area of the Earth's surface, inside the black shadow or **umbra** that is cast by the Moon. This umbra is only a few hundred miles across. Around this is a less shadowy area, called the **penumbra**.

The diagram above shows how the Moon blocks out the Sun's light during an eclipse. A total eclipse can only be seen from within the umbra. From the penumbra you would only see a partial eclipse.

An eclipse takes place in a series of stages. The Moon takes about two hours to pass right across the face of the Sun, but the total part, when the Sun is completely hidden, may last only for a very few minutes.

FUTURE ECLIPSES

Date	Length of Totality	Where Visible
1990 Jul. 22	2½ min.	Finland, Soviet Union, Pacific
1991 Jul. 11	7 min.	Pacific, Central America, Brazil
1992 Jun. 30	5½ min.	South Atlantic
1994 Nov. 3	4½ min.	Peru, Brazil, South Atlantic
1995 Oct. 24	2 min.	Near East, India, Pacific
1997 Mar. 9	3 min.	Soviet Union, Arctic
1998 Feb. 26	4 min.	Pacific, Central America, Atlantic
1999 Aug. 11	2½ min.	Atlantic, Britain, Europe, India

A curtain of light

The future appearance of eclipses can be worked out for hundreds of years ahead. But another event connected with the Sun, an **aurora**, cannot. Auroras are caused by atomic particles sprayed out from the Sun's surface in areas where there are sunspots, at speeds of more than 600 miles a second.

These particles are attracted by **magnetism**, and the metal in the Earth's core behaves like a huge magnet, which is why compass needles always point north and south. The magnetic power of the Earth reaches outward into space, forming an area around it known as a "magnetic field." When the particles sent out by the Sun come close to Earth, the magnetic field pulls them into the atmosphere at the North and South **Poles**.

At a height of 90 miles or more above the Earth's surface, the particles begin to strike atoms of oxygen and nitrogen near the top of the atmosphere. This causes the atoms to glow green or red, and sometimes other colors as well, so that people living in lands far to the north or south of the Earth's equator will see their night sky lit up with these glowing colors.

Some auroras are seen as just a faint greenish glow. Others have the appearance of a curtain of light shimmering in front of the stars. Every now and then an aurora can be so strong that it sweeps brilliant colored rays like searchlights across the sky.

Bright auroras are most often seen when a large sunspot group appears on the Sun's face. This means that they are most common when the **sunspot cycle** is at a maximum. Some good displays can be expected in the early 1990s, when sunspots will be plentiful again.

The diagram below shows how streams of particles, called the solar wind, continually spread outward from the Sun. The Earth's magnetic field pulls these particles toward its poles. When the solar wind carries particularly strong bursts of particles, sprayed out from sunspots, they make the Earth's upper atmosphere glow. The effect is often beautiful, as in the example of a "curtain" aurora above.

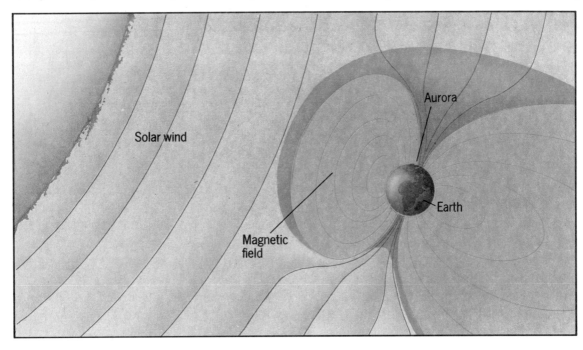

Solar wind

Aurora

Magnetic field

Earth

The aging Sun

Since the beginning of life on the Earth, some 3.5 billion years ago, the Sun has shone more or less steadily. It was once thought that such worldwide events as the sudden extinction of the dinosaurs happened because the Sun cooled down for a time. But it is more likely that the dinosaurs were wiped out by changes in the Earth's atmosphere — possibly an asteroid struck the Earth, pouring dark dust into the atmosphere and shrouding the surface from the Sun, so that plants faded and died, and there was no food for large grazing animals like most of the dinosaurs.

From a swollen giant ...

The Sun is an average sort of star, and uses up its hydrogen "fuel" much more slowly than some very hot and bright stars. But eventually it will come to a "fuel crisis" — in about 5 billion years' time, the brilliant core of helium will have swollen so much that it will begin to collapse, with violent results. At first the core will grow still hotter, and its heat will drive the remaining surface layers of hydrogen outward, making them expand into a vast orange-red ball — a red **giant star**.

This will be a horrifying event for anyone left on the Earth. The inner planet Mercury will vanish inside a roasting mist. Venus may do the same. The Earth itself may not be engulfed, but certainly it will be fried to a cinder. Its air will be blasted away and its oceans boiled dry — it will be a red-hot, lifeless ball of rock.

... to a tiny dwarf

The red giant stage will probably last for several billion years, but eventually there will be no more hydrogen fuel left around the core. The red mist of hydrogen will drift off into space, leaving the shrunken core as a minute hot star about the same size as the Earth. It will have become a white **dwarf star**, containing most of the material the Sun does now but shrunk to about one millionth of its present size. A matchbox-sized sample of a white dwarf, if it could somehow be put on a set of scales, would weigh several tons!

It will be possible to see the stars once more in the Earth's sky, but a visiting astronaut, arriving on the dead, rocky landscape of Earth, under a sun giving no more light than our present full Moon, could be forgiven for doubting if life-forms had ever existed here. Slowly, over more millions of years, our dying star will become even dimmer as it changes color from white to yellow to red, finally leaving its planets in total darkness.

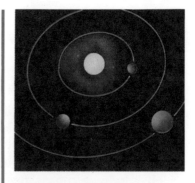

Today the Sun is a yellowish-white star, as it has been for about 4.6 billion years. For most of this time, there has been life on Earth.

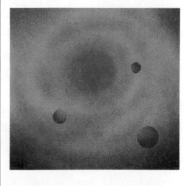

In 5 billion years, the Sun will begin to turn into a red giant. It will swallow the inner planets, and the Earth will be roasted. Even Mars will bake under this Sun.

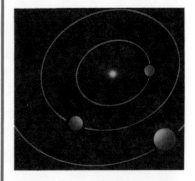

After another 5 billion years, the red-giant Sun will have changed again. Now the planets orbit a dim, shrunken star, no bigger than the Earth, which is slowly fading into darkness.

Today, the Sun shines just strongly enough to let life on the Earth exist in its present state. A little cooler and the oceans would freeze. A little warmer and the planet would become like a stifling greenhouse. We think our world is normal, but really it is the most "abnormal" planet of all.

Billions of years into the future, things will begin to change. The Sun will start to swell and grow hotter. The oceans will turn into steam, and all life-forms will die in the smothering heat. For a time, the atmosphere may be so thick that the Sun is invisible.

When the Sun reaches the red giant stage, the Earth's surface will bake dry and the atmosphere will leak away into space. The "day" side of the planet will be hotter than an oven, scorched by the vast red Sun. Even at night, the sky may be tinged red. Our planet will be a cinder.

Finally, the Sun will become a tiny pinpoint, casting its silvery light over a frozen landscape. The stars will shine brightly in the black sky. Most or all of the stars known to us now will have faded away, and new stars and new solar systems, perhaps with life-forms of their own, will have taken their place.

4. The Planets

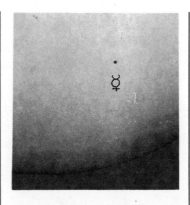

On rare occasions, Mercury passes between the Earth and the Sun, and appears as a tiny black spot moving across the Sun's face in a few hours. This is known as a "transit." The last transit of Mercury happened on November 13, 1986, and the next two will be in 1993 and 1999. This picture shows how Mercury appeared at the transit of May 9, 1970. The planet's black dot is marked here with the ancient Greek symbol for Mercury.

Mercury

Mercury is the innermost planet, and always appears very close to the Sun in the sky. It is sometimes noticeable as a twinkling "star" in the dawn or evening twilight, but very little was known about what it was like as a world until 1974. Then the space probe Mariner 10 took the first close-up photographs.

Mercury is an airless globe less than half the diameter of the Earth, with a surface crowded with craters. Because there is no atmosphere to reflect the light of the Sun, the sky is always black, like the sky on the Moon or out in space. Perhaps the most unusual thing about Mercury is that the length of its day is longer than its year! It orbits the Sun once in 88 days (its year), but someone standing on the surface watching the Sun slowly set would have to wait for 176 Earth days before the Sun set again at the end of the next Mercurian day.

A hot and cold planet

Not surprisingly, the surface becomes very hot when the Sun is high in the sky — it reaches about 660 degrees, which is the temperature of an ordinary oven set for baking a cake. But since there is no atmosphere to hold some of the heat in during the night, the midnight surface temperature is freezing cold — about 270 degrees below zero, which is about the same as the cloud temperature of distant Jupiter. Strangely enough the ground inside some of the craters very near to Mercury's poles may never receive any direct sunlight at all, and must be among the coldest places in the solar system, even though Mercury is the closest planet to the Sun.

The Mariner 10 space probe was put into orbit around the Sun, and passed Mercury three times in 1974 and 1975. It gave astronomers the only close-up photographs of Mercury they have so far had before its instruments stopped working.

Mariner also discovered that Mercury has a huge iron core, probably about three-fourths the size of the planet itself.

MERCURY FACTS

Average distance from Sun: 36 million miles
Nearest distance from Earth: 28 million miles
Temperature on sunlit side: 660 degrees
Temperature on dark side: −270 degrees
Diameter across equator: 3,030 miles
Atmosphere: None
Number of moons: 0
Length of day: 176 Earth days
Length of year: 88 Earth days

Earth —
Mercury —

49

Venus is covered with an atmosphere of unbreathable carbon dioxide, which is so thick that to walk on the ground would be more like swimming. Droplets of sulfuric acid, which can eat through both metal and people's skin, rain down from the dark clouds above. Even by day, the land is in a deep reddish twilight. The temperature is higher than on Mercury, staying at about 900 degrees.

Venus

Sweltering Venus is what the Earth would have become if our orbit carried us a little closer to the Sun. The Earth once had a thick steamy atmosphere, but it cooled down enough to fall as rain and fill the oceans. On warmer Venus, however, the steamy clouds remained.

Clouds are good at holding in the heat — a clear night is usually colder than a cloudy one. This meant that the temperature on Venus rapidly rose, and the fierce heat baked poisonous gases, especially carbon dioxide, out of the rocks. Carbon dioxide is one of the best "heat blankets" there is, and as more and more of it escaped into the atmosphere the temperature rose yet again.

We cannot see through the clouds covering Venus, but radar maps show three large highland regions that are completely surrounded by deserts.

The Soviet landing probe Venera 12 visited the surface of Venus in 1975 and sent back photographs of its surroundings. Beneath its clouds of acid, the gloomy surface is rocky and mountainous. The sky of Venus is probably lit up by constant lightning.

The Morning Star

Venus is often known as the Morning Star or the Evening Star, since it may either rise in our sky before the Sun in the east, or set after it in the west. Venus looks so bright and silvery in our sky because of its clouds, which reflect the Sun's light back into space almost as well as a mirror. In fact, it is the brightest object in the sky after the Sun and the Moon.

The best time to look at Venus is when the sky is still bright blue, because it dazzles the eye when the sky is dark. If you look at Venus through a pair of binoculars, you may be able to see it looking like a very small Moon, showing just the part of it that is lit up by the Sun. This is called its phase. Venus is so bright that it can even be seen without binoculars in full daylight, if you know exactly where to look. There are also plenty of cases of people mistaking the planet for a flying saucer or UFO (Unidentified Flying Object).

From the Earth, we have an almost edge-on view of the orbit of Venus. As it travels around the Sun, we see different amounts of its sunlit surface. These are known as its "phases." It looks much larger when it is just a crescent shape, as this is when it is closest to Earth. When we see the whole of its daylight face, it is on the far side of its orbit.

VENUS FACTS

Average distance from Sun: 67 million miles
Nearest distance from Earth: 26 million miles
Average temperature: 900 degrees
Diameter across equator: 7,523 miles
Atmosphere: Mainly carbon dioxide
Number of moons: 0
Length of day: 8.3 Earth years
Length of year: 225 Earth days

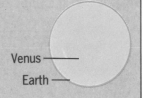

Venus —

Earth —

The Earth

The Earth, our own planet, is special in many ways. It is rocky, but it also has plenty of water; it has clouds, but it also has clear sky. All the other planets of the solar system are either rock or ice, cloudy or airless. The Earth is in a delicate balance, and this balance has allowed life to develop here.

The Earth has turned out like this because it happens to be the right distance away from the Sun. Just a little bit closer, and it would have turned into a choking Venus — a little bit farther away, and it would have been a barren frozen Mars.

The inside of the Earth seems to be special, too. A hard surface crust, about 25 miles thick, "floats" on hot molten rock beneath, and earthquakes and volcanic eruptions prove that there is plenty of heat and activity below the surface. The other inner planets seem to be much "quieter" in comparison. The Earth also has a stronger magnetic field than the other rocky planets.

Most importantly, it teems with life. If you tested a spoonful of almost any part of our planet — air, water, earth, or rock — with a microscope, it would show you tiny living organisms by the million. So far, our exploration of space has revealed no other life anywhere else.

Since it was first possible to see the Earth from space, it has been known as the "blue and white" planet. Both colors are caused by the presence of water — the blue comes from the oceans, and the white comes from clouds of water droplets or ice crystals in the atmosphere. The Earth is the most brightly colored object in the solar system.

The Sun and the Earth

Without the Sun, the Earth's surface would be dark and frozen. It brings light and warmth to help plants and animals grow. But different parts of the Earth warm up at a different rate. In the daytime, the land areas become hotter than the sea, but at night they cool more quickly.

If there were no seas, the Earth would get much hotter during the day and much colder at night. Even now, the parts of the Earth near the North and South Poles are always frozen. This is because the Sun is never high in the sky in these regions, and the sunlight is not strong enough to warm the icy ground.

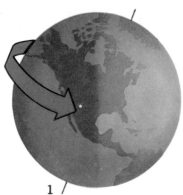
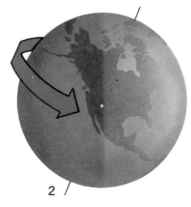
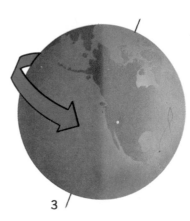

1 /   2 /   3 /

As the Earth turns, the Sun shines on different parts of our world.
1. When the east coast of the United States is in full daylight, the west coast is still in darkness.
2. As dawn breaks over the Grand Canyon in the south-western state of Arizona, the Sun has already risen over half the country.
3. By the time morning arrives in the Grand Canyon, it is nearly lunchtime for people on the east coast.

The Earth spins once in 24 hours. In this time the Sun rises in the east and sets in the west, giving us day and night. Dawn begins some time before sunrise, when the first rays of the Sun are reflected off atoms and small dust particles in the high atmosphere, causing a glow. If the Earth had no atmosphere, there would be no dawn — the blinding Sun would appear almost without warning above the horizon.

Sometimes the rising or setting Sun seems dim enough to stare at, because the atmosphere blocks out some of its light. Do not take the risk. Invisible heat rays may still hurt your eyes, even though you cannot feel them.

EARTH FACTS

Average distance from Sun: 93 million miles
Temperature on sunlit side: 77 degrees (average)
Temperature on dark side: 59 degrees (average)
Diameter across equator: 7,928 miles
Atmosphere: Nitrogen 78%, oxygen 21%
Number of moons: 1
Length of day: 24 hours
Length of year: 365.25 days

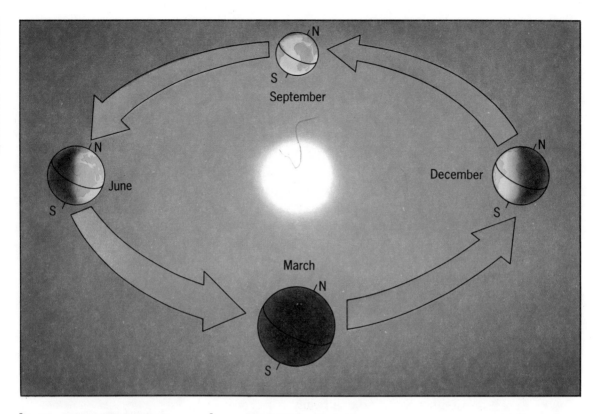

September

June

December

March

The Earth's axis always leans in the same direction. In June, the northern half or hemisphere of the planet is in summer because it is leaning toward the Sun. It receives more warmth and daylight than the southern hemisphere, which is in midwinter.

Six months later, in December, the Earth has gone halfway around the Sun. The southern hemisphere is now in midsummer, while the northern hemisphere is in midwinter. However, in March and September both hemispheres have an equal share of day and night.

A tilted Earth

Imagine the Earth as a table tennis ball with a pointed stick pushed through the middle of it. This stick would be its **axis**. But the axis will not be perfectly upright as the Earth follows its orbit around the Sun. In fact, it is tilted from the upright at an angle of 23 degrees, which is about a quarter of a right angle (90 degrees).

This small tilt of the Earth's axis has a very important effect upon the weather and, therefore, upon everything that lives on our planet. It means that in the course of each year the Sun is sometimes high up in the sky during its daily journey from east to west, and sometimes much lower down. When it is high, the days are longer and hotter than when it is low. This is why we have the **seasons** of spring, summer, autumn, and winter.

Alternative seasons

This tilt of the axis is another interesting piece of "chance." If the axis were perfectly upright, every month would be the same. Trees and flowers would always be in leaf and bloom, or else we would have no trees and flowers at all!

Another possibility is even more alarming — if the axis were tilted right on its side, at 90 degrees, each half of the Earth would have six months of continuous day in summer, and six months of continuous night in winter. Living things would have to move from one half of the world or hemisphere to the other, chasing the sunlight and warmth in order to survive.

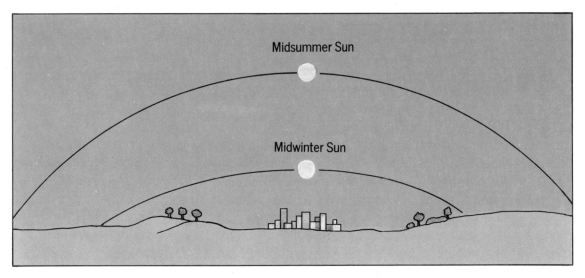

Timing the Sun

From Earth, the Sun appears to pass across our sky from sunrise to sunset, although of course it is the Earth that is really moving, not the Sun. The Sun is highest in the sky exactly halfway between rising and setting, a time known as "noon." If you look for the direction of the Sun at noon, it will be due south if you are living in Europe, the northern United States, or Canada, but due north if you are in Australia or New Zealand.

A simple way of discovering when it is noon, without looking at a watch, is to draw a line pointing north and south on the ground and to set an upright stick on it. Noon is when the stick's shadow lies along the line.

Noon is not always at exactly 12 o'clock, because most countries use an "average" or Mean Time. For example, noon in eastern New York state is actually about a quarter of an hour before noon in western New York, but clocks and watches in both places show the same time.

The midwinter Sun always passes lower across the sky than the midsummer Sun, and it rises later and sets sooner. This means that the winter day is shorter as well as colder. In ancient times, people noticed that the Sun rose above different points on the horizon at different times of the year, and used this knowledge to make a calendar.

MAKING A SUNDIAL

On a sunny morning, fix a straight stick in the ground. Every hour, place a marker on the ground at the tip of the stick's shadow. Notice how the shadow shortens as noon approaches, and then lengthens again. Try to decide just when the shadow was shortest. Did your "sundial" noon agree with "clock" noon? Remember, daylight saving time is an hour ahead of "sundial" time.

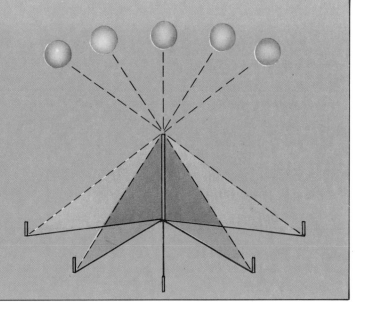

Earth's atmosphere

If you think of the Earth as the size of an orange, the layer of atmosphere around it is far thinner than the peel. Yet this is enough both to allow life to develop and to protect it. It keeps us warm and damp, shields us from dangerous rays sent out by the Sun, and lets plants and animals breathe.

The Earth's atmosphere must have changed a lot since the planet was formed. To begin with it was probably mostly carbon dioxide gas (this contains carbon and oxygen atoms and is given out by volcanoes that must then have spouted everywhere), water vapor, and nitrogen gas. As the surface of the Earth cooled down, the water vapor cooled as well and fell as rain, creating the oceans. Most of the carbon dioxide dissolved in the water, leaving the atmosphere with plenty of nitrogen and only a little carbon dioxide.

The arrival of life

It could have remained like that until the present time, if the first simple plant cells had not started to develop. These take in carbon dioxide, using the carbon to build more cells, and give back the oxygen to the air. Gradually oxygen gas built up in the atmosphere, and animals, which need a supply of oxygen to breathe, could develop. It is the green plants growing everywhere that have given the Earth its unique oxygen atmosphere.

Oxygen also protects life on the Earth. High up in the atmosphere there is a thin layer of ozone. This is a form of oxygen that blocks off lethal rays that come from the Sun. If the ozone layer were removed we should suffer severe sunburn and die, as astronauts would if they were not shielded by thick spacesuits or the walls of their spacecraft.

The atmosphere can be divided into different "layers," each one thicker than the one above. Thin traces of atmospheric gases have been found as high as 600 miles above the surface, but half of all the gases are below the height of Mount Everest (29,000 feet). This layer is known as the "troposphere."

The next layer is the "stratosphere." Aircrafts fly in the stratosphere, but the cabins need to be filled with air, because there is not enough for people to breathe. The vital ozone layer is also in the stratosphere, at a height of about 25 miles.

Above the stratosphere is the "mesosphere," then the "ionosphere," where auroras are seen.

The photograph at the top of the page shows how the atmosphere looks from space — a thin colored band surrounding the Earth.

THE WEIGHT OF AIR

To see how strongly the atmosphere presses down on us, ask an adult to boil a little water in a loosely capped metal container; take it off the heat, and carefully tighten the cap. The steam inside condenses, leaving an airless vacuum, and the pressure of the air outside crushes the can.

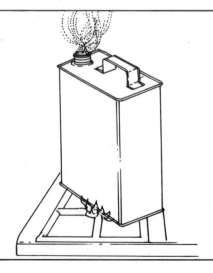
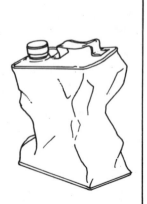

First manned space
flight (230 miles)

Aurora

Ionosphere

Mesosphere

Ozone layer

Aircraft

Stratosphere

Troposphere

The Earth and the Moon are close companions, but they are very different worlds. The cratered Moon looks like the planet Mercury, or some of the satellites of the outer planets. Its surface has remained almost unchanged for more than 3 billion years — since life first appeared upon the Earth.

Earth's satellite

Why are the Moon and the Earth so different? They were probably formed at about the same time, out of the same cloud of material. But the Earth is blue and white and teeming with life, while the Moon is a cratered fossil.

The reason is their size. The Moon is a fourth of the Earth's diameter, and its gravity is only one-sixth as strong. This did two things. First, its crust set solid much more quickly than the Earth's, since a small body cools faster than a large one. Second, the gases in its atmosphere were too light for its weak gravity to hold down, and they floated off into space.

When flying rock from space blasted huge craters in its surface, the Moon was not able to wear them down with weather, or rub them out with its moving crust. It was a big ball of cold stone. Only the dark dry plains known as "seas" show where molten rock or "lava" flowed out from beneath the crust and covered some of the craters.

The Moon lightens our nights by reflecting sunlight. It is 100 times closer to the Earth than any planet, and 400 times closer than the Sun itself.

MOON FACTS

Least distance from Earth: 224,363 miles

Average distance from Earth: 237,415 miles

Greatest distance from Earth: 250,466 miles

Temperature on sunlit side: 212 degrees

Temperature on dark side: −270 degrees

Diameter across equator: 2,160 miles

Atmosphere: None

Length of day: 27.3 Earth days

Length of year: 1 Earth year

Length of lunar month: 29.5 Earth days

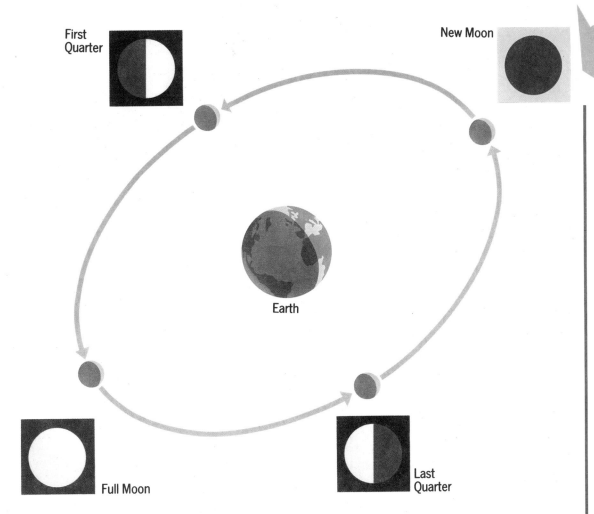

First Quarter

New Moon

Sun's light

Earth

Full Moon

Last Quarter

The phases of the Moon

The Sun can shine on only half of the Moon at a time, leaving the rest of the globe dark and invisible. As the Moon goes around the Earth, we see this sunlit half from different angles, known as phases — sometimes as a thin sliver or crescent, and at other times as a round Full Moon.

It takes a "lunar month" of about 29.5 days for the Moon to go through all its phases. The time of New Moon signals the beginning of the lunar month. Many people call the slim crescent seen in the evening sky the New Moon, but the real New Moon is completely invisible to us unless it passes directly in front of the Sun, producing an eclipse.

Gradually, our view of the bright part of the Moon grows until exactly half of the sunlight side is visible a week after New Moon. This phase is often called First Quarter because the Moon has now passed along a quarter of its orbit. Full Moon follows a week later, when the whole of the sunlit side points toward the Earth. Then the Moon shrinks again to another half, or Last Quarter, and finally vanishes again.

This diagram shows how the Moon passes through its phases. Our view of the Moon is shown in the square alongside each phase.

New Moon: The whole of the sunlit side of the Moon is hidden from our view, and the side of the Moon facing Earth is in darkness.

First Quarter: As the Moon moves around the Earth, half of its sunlit side can be seen after sunset.

Full Moon: This rises as the Sun sets because it is opposite the Sun in our sky.

Last Quarter: The Moon now rises late in the night and is still high in the sky at dawn.

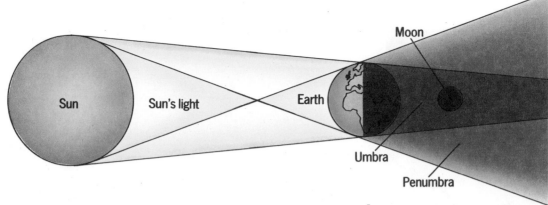

Moon

Sun

Sun's light

Earth

Umbra

Penumbra

In the Earth's shadow

The Earth casts a tapering shadow in space more than a half million miles long, pointing away from the Sun. When the Moon is full, there is about one chance in ten that it will pass through the Earth's shadow, and be darkened by it or eclipsed.

When this happens, we first of all see the Moon with a smoky haze growing over one side of it. Then a dark "bite" appears as the Moon moves into the full shadow. After an hour, if the eclipse is a total one, the Moon will have turned a dark reddish-brown color.

Usually it can be seen even when the eclipse is total, because the atmosphere around the Earth acts like a lens, and "bends" some of the sunlight into the shadow, turning it a deep red color.

Sometimes, however, the Moon disappears entirely. This happened during an eclipse in December 1982, when observers could not even find it using binoculars! The reason for this was that clouds of dust particles had been thrown high into the atmosphere by the Mexican volcano El Chichon earlier that year. The dust blocked out all the sunlight from the Earth's shadow. By the next total eclipse, in 1985, the shadow was normal again.

This diagram shows how the Moon is eclipsed if it passes through the Earth's dark central shadow or umbra. If it passes through the lighter outer shadow or penumbra, the effect on the Moon is not likely to be noticed.

If you were standing on the Moon during a lunar eclipse, you would see it as an eclipse of the Sun. The Earth, looking four times the size of the Sun, would appear as a huge black disk blocking off all the Sun's light except for a reddish halo caused by its atmosphere.

ECLIPSES OF THE MOON
The next eclipses of the Moon will be as follows:

1988	Aug. 27 Partial	**1990**	Aug. 6 Partial
1989	Feb. 20 Total	**1991**	Dec. 21 Partial
1989	Aug. 17 Total	**1992**	June. 15 Partial
1990	Feb. 9 Total	**1992**	Dec. 10 Total

The Moon and tides

Everything in the universe has gravity. Gravity is what keeps the planets orbiting the Sun, and it is the Earth's gravity that keeps the Moon circling around the Earth. But the Moon also pulls on the Earth. Its gravity tugs at the water in our oceans and makes them bulge outward, as shown in picture 1 on the right.

These bulges are only a few feet high, but as the Earth spins they move around the oceans, lifting first one part and then another. This is why the sea appears to go up and down every twelve hours, and why we have **tides**.

The Sun's gravity is hundreds of times stronger than the Moon's, but it feels weaker to us because it is so far away. It also raises tides on the Earth, but these are much smaller than the Moon's (picture 2). If the Moon and the Sun are in line with the Earth, which happens at New Moon and Full Moon, they both pull together on the oceans and we get very high tides, called spring tides (picture 3). When the Sun and Moon are at right angles to each other, at First Quarter and Last Quarter, they pull in different directions and we get very weak tides, called neap tides (picture 4).

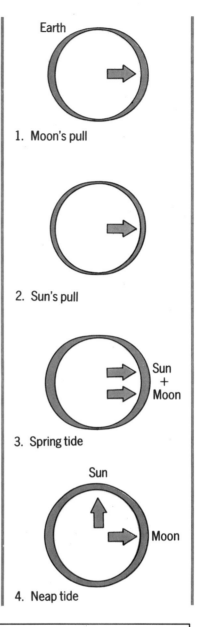

Earth

1. Moon's pull

2. Sun's pull

Sun + Moon

3. Spring tide

Sun

Moon

4. Neap tide

THE MOON'S FACE

When the Moon was newly formed it was made of molten rock, spinning around once in a few hours. As it cooled, a hard skin or crust formed on the outside. The Earth's gravity, pulling at this crust, slowed the spin down and raised a "bulge" a few miles high on one side. Now this bulge is always turned inward, and the Moon keeps the same face toward the Earth.

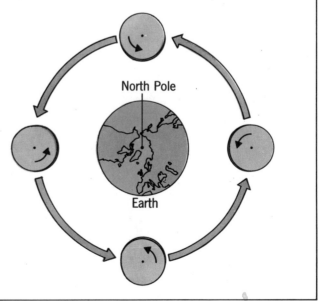

North Pole

Earth

How the Moon was formed

The Moon was formed in the same way as the Earth — by countless small solid objects colliding together and building up into a larger one. When two objects hit each other a lot of heat is given out. With the number of objects hitting the growing Moon, there was enough heat to make it molten.

Gradually, the number of collisions slowed down, the Moon began to cool, and a thin crust formed. This meant that marks of later collisions did not just melt away and disappear, but remained as huge hollows or craters.

A crater is not the size of the object that made it, but marks the explosion the object made. A rock one mile across, hitting the hard lunar surface at a speed of about 50 miles a second, will explode like an enormous bomb, blasting a crater ten times its size. Some very large craters even show rings or ripples in the rock surrounding them, caused by the shock waves.

If you drop a pebble into water and watch carefully, you will see a little mound jump up in the middle of the splash. This is another shock wave, and explains why some craters have a mountain at the center.

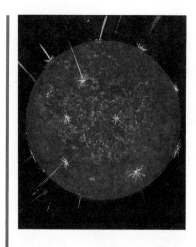

At first, the newborn Moon must have been a red-hot globe of rock, whirling through a hail of dust and rocky particles inside the solar nebula. Gradually the "storm" lessened and the surface hardened about 3.9 billion years ago.

Once the Moon's surface grew cool and hard, later collisions left huge marks in the rock.
1. When an object hit the surface it would explode like a bomb.
2. This formed a crater much larger than the object.
3. Later collisions would partly overlap the first crater, blurring its shape.

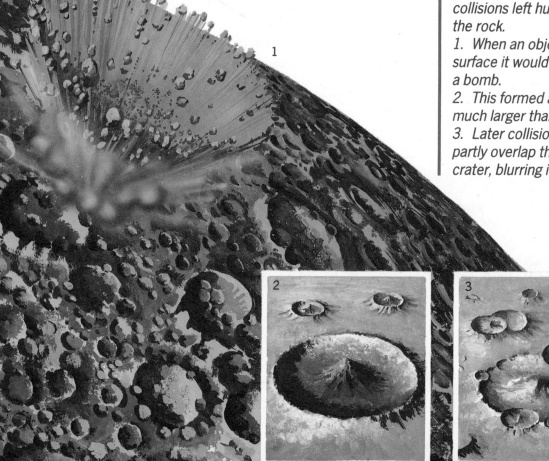

1

This photograph of the Moon was taken by the Apollo 11 astronauts. The left side is part of the hemisphere that we always see from the Earth, while the right-hand side is part of the hemisphere that is always turned away. It had never been seen until the Soviet spacecraft Luna 3 sent back a photograph in 1959.

The side turned away from the Earth was found to have hardly any dark areas or "seas." This seems to prove that the pull of the Earth helped to crack the surface to allow molten lava to flood out, producing the seas on the side facing Earth.

The Moon today

Stray pieces of rock continued to collide with the planets and their satellites long after they had been fully formed. Many of the craters we see on the Moon now are from these later collisions, up to about 3.9 billion years ago. Some of these craters are enormous — large enough to contain several cities as big as New York, and with mountains higher than the Alps rising up from their floors. Over the years, astronomers have made maps of the Moon's surface, giving names to most of the larger craters and to the smooth, dark patches on the Moon known as "seas."

Rock samples that were collected from the Moon by the Apollo astronauts were found to have melted and formed over 4 billion years ago. This proves that most of the Moon's surface has not changed in any important way since that time. On the Earth's surface pieces of rock as old as 3 billion years are very rare, because most of the surface is slowly rising or sinking as the ages pass.

The "seas," however, must have formed after this date, as even binoculars show that there are not many craters on them. This is because the old craters were flooded by the lava that poured out from cracks in the Moon's surface and formed the "seas." It flowed over the old craters, leaving the surface much smoother and flatter when it cooled.

Man on the Moon

Between 1969 and the end of 1972, a number of Apollo spacecrafts were sent to the Moon. One, Apollo 13, had a malfunction on the way out and had to return to Earth. The other six each landed two astronauts safely on the Moon, and these twelve lunar explorers brought back enough rock and dust samples to fill about six large knapsacks. From these samples we have discovered a lot about the age of the Moon and what it is made of.

The first plans for Apollo were announced on May 25, 1961, when President Kennedy declared that the United States would land someone on the Moon within the next ten years. This was a bold prediction, because at this point the U.S. had not even put an astronaut into orbit.

The Apollo spacecrafts were all built in two parts — the Command Module and the Landing Module. The Command Module stayed in orbit around the Moon and sent two of its three crew members down to the Moon in the Landing Module. After returning to orbit again, the Landing Module was left behind. Only a part of the Command Module, just large enough for the three astronauts and their treasures, returned to the Earth, floating down into the Atlantic Ocean supported by three parachutes.

The Landing Module from Apollo 11 (called Eagle) begins its descent to the lunar surface about 60 miles below. Most of Eagle remained on the Moon — only the tiny cabin part took off from the surface to bring the two explorers back to the Command Module.

In the far distance, the half-phase Earth shines blue and white in the black sky, against the dark grays and browns of the Moon. The astronauts on all the journeys told how colorful the Earth appeared.

APOLLO LANDINGS

Mission	Date of Landing	Length of Landing	Crew
Apollo 11	July 20, 1969	21½ hrs.	Armstrong/Aldrin
Apollo 12	Nov. 19, 1969	31½ hrs.	Conrad/Bean
Apollo 14	Feb. 5, 1971	33½ hrs.	Shepard/Mitchell
Apollo 15	July 30, 1971	67 hrs.	Scott/Irwin
Apollo 16	April 21, 1972	71 hrs.	Young/Duke
Apollo 17	Dec. 11, 1972	75 hrs.	Cernan/Schmitt

The Apollo explorers

The astronauts making the first three Apollo landings had to explore the Moon by foot. The last three spacecrafts carried a Lunar Rover, a battery-powered car. Gasoline engines will not work on the Moon because there is no air to make the gasoline burn.

The most important task of all was to collect samples of rock and dust to bring back to Earth. The astronauts had to use scoops to collect the dust samples, since their spacesuits were too stiff for them to bend or kneel. They used a hammer to chip pieces of rock off large boulders.

They also set up experiments that would keep on working after they had left the Moon, and would send the results back by radio. One of these recorded moonquakes. Another measured the temperature deep inside the ground.

The crew of Apollo 12 landed their craft near an unmanned lunar probe, Surveyor 3, that had been sent to the Moon two and a half years previously. They brought parts of the probe back to Earth so that scientists could study them.

One of the astronauts from Apollo 11 inspects the Lunar Module's foot pad. The dust on the Moon's surface is as fine as flour. Without wind or rain to disturb them, the Apollo astronauts' footprints will stay perfectly preserved for centuries.

Harrison Schmitt from Apollo 17 leaves his Lunar Rover to collect a rock sample from a huge boulder. The peculiar looking "umbrella" on the back of the Rover is a radio antenna. The Rover could travel at a maximum speed of 9 mph.

Mars, the red planet

The "red planet" seemed special as soon as the first powerful telescopes were pointed at it. Less than 100 years ago, many people thought intelligent beings might live there. But now, during the past 20 years, space probes have shown that it is a cold desert.

Mars turns out to be a planet of contrasts. Parts of its surface show old craters, like a rather worn-down Moon. Elsewhere there are signs that volcanoes once exploded with floods of lava, although there are no signs of ancient volcanoes on the Moon. Mars is only half the size of the Earth, but its features are much grander. Its surface must have been torn apart by early upheavals.

That surface now freezes beneath an atmosphere nearly a hundred times thinner than our own. It is possible that the surface was once warmer — some deep channels look as if water once ran in them. But all its water is now frozen to ice somewhere beneath the dusty deserts and, as space probes have discovered, there are no definite signs of any form of life.

Two Viking probes visited Mars in 1976. Each one sent a lander down to the surface to study the conditions there. The probe in the picture is viewing the enormous volcanic mountain Olympus Mons. This, the tallest mountain in the solar system, is three times as high as Mount Everest. The surface of Mars is also seamed by huge valleys.

On the left of the picture is Phobos, one of the two tiny moons of Mars. It is an irregular lump of rock about 12 miles across.

MARS FACTS

Average distance from Sun: 142 million miles
Nearest distance from Earth: 48 million miles
Temperature on sunlit side: 32 degrees
Temperature on dark side: −270 degrees
Diameter across equator: 4,220 miles
Atmosphere: Carbon dioxide
Number of moons: 2
Length of day: 24 hours 37 minutes
Length of year: 687 Earth days

Mars————
Earth————

A Martian's claw grasps at a human in the film The War of the Worlds, *made in 1953. When this story was first told on American radio in 1938, there was almost nationwide panic — people were prepared to believe in Martians then. But the only real "claws" on Mars belong to the two Viking landers. The one shown below is Viking 1.*

Although a day on Mars is only half an hour longer than on the Earth, everything else about it is different. Photographs taken by the Viking space probes show that the landscape is red-brown, stony, and desolate. There are strong winds too, and even from the Earth astronomers can sometimes make out huge dust storms blowing over the surface. This dust has turned the Martian sky pink instead of the dark blue that scientists expected to find.

Mars is bitterly cold. Even in summer the air temperature is never above the freezing point, and by sunset the ground is covered with a frost of frozen carbon dioxide about 150 degrees below zero.

Jupiter, the giant

Jupiter is so huge that all the other planets in the solar system could fit inside it, but it also has the shortest day of all — less than ten hours. It is spinning so fast on its axis that it has a slightly squashed appearance. This is because the clouds near the equator are being pushed outward by the speed. Its shape proved that the planet is not solid and rocky long before space probes passed near it.

Jupiter is made of hydrogen but, as described on page 28, this is more like a liquid than a gas. Its dark bands are where other elements such as carbon, nitrogen, and phosphorus float up from below the upper clouds and are pulled into whirls and streaks by the planet's spin. Close-up photographs show amazing blues, greens, and reds in these clouds. They are always changing; even through an amateur astronomer's telescope, Jupiter never looks the same from one night to the next.

This view shows Jupiter and two of its satellites, innermost Io and Europa. The huge cloud known as the Great Red Spot is near the bottom of the planet, just coming into "morning" — in five hours it will be passing into night at the other side of the planet.

Europa, at the far left of the picture, is covered with ice, but Io, which is slightly larger than our own Moon, is the most violent place in the solar system. It is covered with volcanoes.

The Voyager I probe, which passed Jupiter in 1979, found a ring around the planet that astronomers had not known was there. This ring is very narrow and faint, and is probably made up of dust and small pieces of rock. A photograph of Jupiter with a computerized image of its ring added to it is shown below. The real ring is not as bright as this.

JUPITER FACTS

Average distance from Sun: 484 million miles

Nearest distance from Earth: 391 million miles

Average temperature (clouds): −240 degrees

Diameter across equator: 88,751 miles

Atmosphere: Hydrogen, helium

Number of moons: 14 known

Length of day: 9 hours 50 minutes

Length of year: 11.9 Earth years

Earth

Jupiter

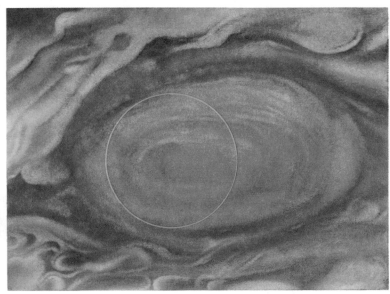

The temperature of the clouds that we can see is about 240 degrees below zero. This is higher than it should be if Jupiter depended for all its warmth on the distant Sun. Therefore, it must be hot inside. In fact, the temperature at the center of Jupiter is probably about 54,000 degrees, or five times hotter than the surface of the Sun!

This means that somewhere between the bitter chill of the surface clouds and the roasting center of the planet, there must be a level where the temperature is bearable for some type of life-form. Perhaps there are living things that exist somewhere, in calmer, sheltered backwaters between the raging clouds of hydrogen, just below the surface layers that we can see.

Jupiter's clouds contain all the ingredients found in living things, and on the Earth microscopic animals can live in strange places — even in boiling water, or in strong chemicals that would be poisonous to humans. We shall know more when the first space probe plunges through the clouds on its one-way journey below the awesome face of the giant planet.

The most famous cloud on Jupiter, the Great Red Spot, is a gigantic whirlpool, larger than the Earth. Drawings of the planet made using primitive telescopes 300 years ago show signs of the Red Spot, so it has lasted far longer than any of the other bright or dark clouds we see on the surface today.

Seeing the size of the Earth, shown here as a blue circle, against the size of the Red Spot gives some idea of the vastness of the whole of Jupiter.

69

Saturn

Known for so long as the "planet with the rings," Saturn is now just one of three planets known to have ring systems. But its rings are by far the brightest and most spectacular. Before space probes visited it, three wide rings were known. These have now been photographed from close up, and instead of being wide sheets of rock and ice particles they turn out to be made up of thousands of narrow ringlets.

There are also other ringlets, both closer to Saturn and farther away, not seen from the Earth. Why Saturn should have so many more rings than the other ringed planets is a mystery.

Saturn's rings are made up of pieces of ice and rock, as well as dust, in ringlets just a few hundred yards wide. They form a perfectly flat band 20 times the diameter of the Earth. To get some idea of their size, remember that the Earth could fit between Saturn and its closest ring. Some tiny moons orbit Saturn in narrow gaps between the rings.

Beneath its thick, foggy atmosphere, the surface of Titan, one of Saturn's moons, may look like the picture shown on the right. Titan could even have some kind of life-forms on it.

The rings of Saturn, as seen from the Earth, sometimes look very narrow and at other times very wide. This happens because the axis of Saturn is tilted, and we see the rings from different angles as it journeys around the Sun during its long orbital "year."

What caused the rings? Perhaps a small moon or two broke up into tiny pieces, or perhaps the particles have been there since the solar system formed.

As well as its rings, more moons have been discovered around Saturn than any other planet. So far, 24 are known to exist. Most are less than 60 miles across, and all have been described as "giant snowballs" because they seem to be thickly covered with ice.

Titan – a "foggy" moon

Perhaps the most interesting moon is the largest, Titan (diameter 3,170 miles), which has an atmosphere twice as thick as the Earth's. The Voyager spacecraft could not see through this foggy atmosphere to photograph the surface, but as it passed Titan it used its instruments to find out what the atmosphere is made of. It turns out to be mostly nitrogen gas — the gas most common in our own air — but another ingredient, methane, was more interesting. Methane, made up of nitrogen and carbon, is found on the Earth as natural gas, which is pumped from under the ground into our homes.

Soon after the Earth formed, its atmosphere may also have contained methane gas. This was before plants and other living things began to breathe it. Some scientists think that methane could be a starting point for creating living things. If so, could the atmosphere of Titan also contain some kind of life-forms?

SATURN FACTS

Average distance from Sun: 889 million miles
Nearest distance from Earth: 796 million miles
Average temperature (clouds): −310 degrees
Diameter across equator: 74,580 miles
Diameter of ring system: 169,049 miles
Atmosphere: Hydrogen, helium
Number of moons: 24 known
Length of day: 10 hours 14 minutes
Length of year: 29.5 Earth years

Earth
Saturn

Uranus

The planet Uranus was the first to be discovered with a telescope. The astronomer William Herschel identified it in 1781 (see page 14). It is so far away that its sunlit disk does not look much bigger than a point of light.

One very interesting fact about Uranus was discovered right away — its axis is tipped over on its side. This means that each pole in turn enjoys continuous sunlight for about 40 Earth years! Not much else was known about it until 1977, when a set of nine narrow rings was found. They are much fainter and more spread out than the rings of Saturn.

The big jump in our knowledge came when Voyager 2 passed the planet and its satellites in January 1986. It found a freezing haze or fog over the planet, and it also measured the length of the planet's day at about 16 hours. The temperature of the cloud surface is 360 degrees below zero, about what astronomers expected. A surprise finding, however, was a thin veil of hydrogen spreading out into space far beyond the cloudy surface.

When Voyager 2 passed Uranus in 1986, it sent back to Earth the most distant messages ever received from a space probe. It was traveling so fast that it had to make all its observations of Uranus and its moons in just a few hours, after a journey that took eight and a half years.

One unusual feature of Uranus is that the tilt of its axis (shown by the red lines) is very extreme.

URANUS FACTS

Average distance from Sun: 1.7 billion miles
Nearest distance from Earth: 1.6 billion miles
Average temperature (clouds): −360 degrees
Diameter across equator: 32,318 km
Atmosphere: Hydrogen, helium
Number of moons: 15 known
Length of day: 16 hours
Length of year: 84 Earth years

Earth
Uranus

William Herschel was an amateur astronomer when he discovered Uranus, along with two of its moons. King George III of England was so pleased with his discovery that he made Herschel a full-time "royal" astronomer.

As it sped past Uranus, Voyager 2 also found four more very narrow rings, making 13 in all, and ten small moons. Even the thickest of these rings are only a few miles wide, and the narrowest are only 500 feet in width. These figures are tiny compared with the diameter of the rings — about 93,000 miles. If you made a model of one of the rings using ordinary string, for example, the loop would have to be about 20 feet across.

Voyager 2 took photographs of the five largest moons of Uranus, showing heavily cratered worlds. Some also have long, deep valleys, and look quite different from the moons of Jupiter and Saturn. Perhaps something strange happened to the moons of Uranus early in their history?

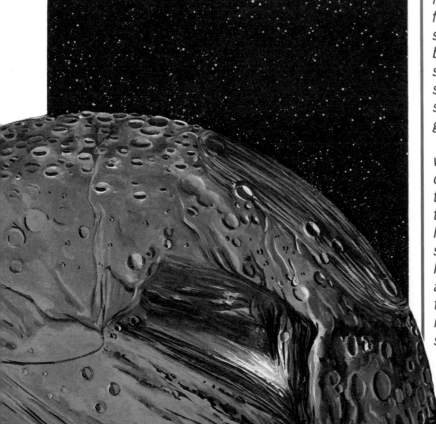

Miranda, the smallest of the five main moons of Uranus, shows features never seen before on any world in the solar system. Experts are still puzzled by the strange, strongly marked sets of grooves in its surface.

It is possible that Miranda was broken apart in a collision, and the pieces then crunched back together, producing these huge ice-wrinkles in its new surface. But what could have broken Miranda apart, and how the pieces came together again, remains a mystery that may never be solved.

The farthest planets

We have learned almost nothing about the outermost hydrogen giant, Neptune, since it was discovered in 1846. It is so far away that no telescope can give even a reasonable view of it. It may be a little smaller than Uranus, but even the length of its day is uncertain. However, it is probably spinning quite rapidly. It is unlikely that our knowledge of Neptune will be improved until Voyager 2 flies past it in August 1989.

Neptune's discovery caused great excitement. Uranus did not seem to be moving along its orbit at the right speed, and two astronomers, John Couch Adams in England and Urbain Leverrier in France, both made up their own minds that an unknown planet's gravity must be tugging at it.

They each set to work to calculate where the new planet must be. Adams finished his calculations first, but British astronomers did not believe them. In the end it was discovered using Leverrier's prediction, which was almost exactly the same as the one worked out by Adams.

Neptune has two moons, Triton and Nereid. Nereid is tiny, but Triton is probably one of the largest moons in the solar system. The picture above shows how we think Neptune would look from the surface of Triton. Earth would be just a dim speck near the starlike Sun.

Urbain Leverrier spent months making tedious calculations by hand that led to the discovery of Neptune. This brilliant piece of work amazed the scientific world, because few people believed that such calculations were possible. Today, the same calculations could be done by a home computer in a few hours.

NEPTUNE FACTS

Average distance from Sun: 2.8 billion miles

Nearest distance from Earth: 2.7 billion miles

Average temperature (clouds): −400 degrees

Diameter across equator: 30,454 miles

Atmosphere: Hydrogen, helium?

Number of moons: 2 known

Length of day: 18–20 hours?

Length of year: 165 Earth years

Earth————

Neptune————

PLUTO FACTS

Average distance from Sun: 3.7 billion miles
Nearest distance from Earth: 3.6 billion miles
Average temperature (clouds): −400 degrees
Diameter across equator: 1,900 miles
Atmosphere: None?
Number of moons: 1 known
Length of day: 6 days 9 hours
Length of year: 248 Earth years

Pluto———
Earth———

Pluto was discovered by the American astronomer Clyde Tombaugh in 1930, after many years of patient searching for a new "Planet X." He took hundreds of photographs of the sky, checking to see if any of the faint "stars" was really a moving planet.

Pluto, the last planet?

What little we know of Pluto tells us that it is a very strange world indeed. It is probably the smallest planet, with a diameter of about 1,900 miles, even smaller than our Moon. It has a very eccentric orbit, which means that sometimes it is almost twice as close to the Sun as at others — in fact, at the present time it is closer than Neptune! Finally, it has a moon, Charon, about half as large as itself, so that many astronomers call them a twin planet rather than a planet with a moon.

We can only guess what Pluto is like, but perhaps both it and Charon are balls of ice with a small rocky core. They move around each other in just less than a week, at a distance about twenty times closer than the gap between the Earth and our Moon. Therefore, although they are both small, they will appear huge and pale in each other's black sky as they spin along the borders of the solar system.

It is even possible that the Sun's family of planets does not end with Pluto's orbit, and there may be other even more remote planets waiting to be found. Only time will give us the answer, because they will probably be discovered by pure luck.

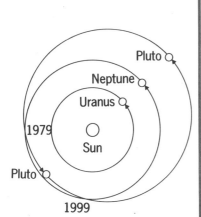

Between 1979 and 1999, Pluto's orbit brings it closer to the Sun than Neptune, so at present, Neptune is the "last" planet.

Pluto and Charon are so close together that they will often produce eclipses of the distant Sun as they orbit each other.

5. The Stars

The moving sky

If you go outside on a clear night, and seat yourself warm and comfortably to watch the stars, you will soon notice that they seem to be moving. Some groups of stars, or constellations, are rising, while others are setting. The night sky is like a huge, slowly spinning hollow ball — a sphere studded with stars, with the Earth at the center.

This view is not a true one. It is the Earth, not the sky, that is spinning. But this idea of a **celestial sphere** is used by astronomers to help "map" the stars in the sky.

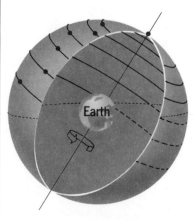

Earth

If you imagine that the stars are fixed to a sphere, which rotates around the Earth, the diagram above shows why half the stars are always invisible, below the horizon.

As the Earth spins, it makes the stars appear to move in circles around the points in space directly above the Earth's axis — the "celestial poles." This photograph was taken by a camera with its lens held open for a long time. It shows the stars near the south celestial pole.

76

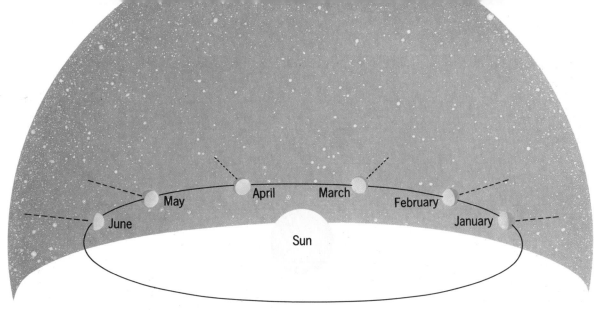

The Earth spins on its axis once in 24 hours, which means that the constellations rise and set once every 24 hours as well. But they cannot all be observed during this time, because some of them are only above the horizon during the daytime.

Fortunately, these "daytime" constellations change during the year, because the Earth is whirling around the Sun like a rider on an amusement park merry-go-round. Imagine that you are the passenger, the center of the machine is the Sun, and the spectators on the ground are the stars. Then, if you keep your eyes on a particular spectator (or star), the center of the merry-go-round (the Sun) will sometimes be opposite the "star" and sometimes pass in front of it.

Seasonal stars

Our view of the Sun against the background of stars, as we orbit around it every year, changes in the same way. This is shown in the diagram above. In January, for example, stars at the right-hand side of the celestial sphere are in good view, because the night side of the Earth is facing toward them. If you imagine yourself looking up at the sky at midnight, these are the stars you will see. But stars at the left-hand side will be invisible, because they are facing the daylight side of the Earth, when the sky is too bright for any stars to be seen.

By June, the position of the Earth is completely different. It has gone around almost half its orbit. Now the stars at the right-hand side of the picture face the sunlit side of the Earth and are invisible, while the ones at the left-hand side may be seen in the night sky.

This is why people speak of "summer" constellations and "winter" constellations. The well-known constellation of Orion, for example, is high in the midnight sky in January, but in July it cannot be seen at all, because the Earth's movement has carried the Sun in front of it.

Stars can only be seen when they shine out in the night sky, even though they are also above the horizon during the day. This means that the best time to look for a particular star is during the time of year when it is on the opposite side of the Earth from the Sun.

An antique model of the celestial sphere, which can be moved to show which stars are above the horizon at any particular time. These models were once used for navigation.

The constellations

Long before people had any idea what the stars are, they had separated them into 48 different groups or constellations. They saw the shapes of animals and figures from myths in the star groups, and this is why we have constellations with names like the Great Bear, or Pegasus, the mythological flying horse. Old maps often had a picture of the object each constellation was meant to represent, drawn over the stars. Modern maps do not do this, because the pictures can hide the star patterns.

We still recognize the same constellations today, because the star patterns have not changed over thousands of years. However, it is important to remember that the stars in a constellation are not really connected in any way — some are probably ten times nearer the Earth than others are.

Even when astronomers learned more about the stars, the constellations were still found to be a useful way of identifying them, and more groups have been added. There are now 88 constellations in the sky, some very large (like the Great Bear) and others, such as Crux (the Cross), very small.

The brighter stars in each constellation are identified by a Greek letter — for example, the brightest star in Leo (the Lion) is Alpha Leonis ("Alpha of the Lion"). Bright stars may also have their own name — Alpha Leonis is also called Regulus, Latin for "the king."

Ancient watchers of the skies traced the shape of Leo, the Lion, in this group of bright stars.

Leo is in the northern half of the celestial sphere. Many of the newer constellations are in the southern half, since they were named when the first voyagers sailed to southern lands in the 16th and 17th centuries.

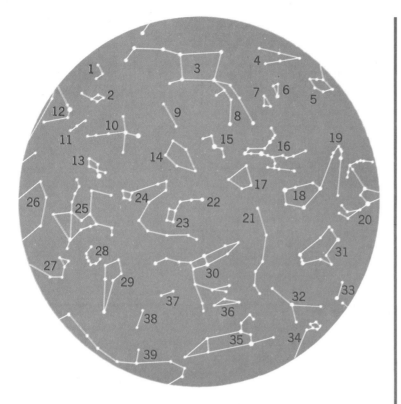

1. Equuleus, the Little Horse
2. Delphinus, the Dolphin
3. Pegasus
4. Pisces, the Fishes
5. Cetus, the Sea Monster
6. Aries, the Ram
7. Triangulum, the Triangle
8. Andromeda
9. Lacerta, the Lizard
10. Cygnus, the Swan
11. Sagitta, the Arrow
12. Aquila, the Eagle
13. Lyra, the Lyre
14. Cepheus
15. Cassiopeia
16. Perseus
17. Camelopardalis, the Giraffe
18. Auriga, the Charioteer
19. Taurus, the Bull
20. Orion
21. Lynx, the Lynx
22. (Polaris, the Pole Star)
23. Ursa Minor, the Little Bear
24. Draco, the Dragon
25. Hercules
26. Ophiuchus, the Serpent-bearer
27. Serpens, the Serpent
28. Corona Borealis, the Northern Crown
29. Bootes, the Herdsman
30. Ursa Major, the Great Bear or Plow
31. Gemini, the Twins
32. Cancer, the Crab
33. Canis Minor, the Little Dog
34. Hydra, the Water Snake
35. Leo, the Lion
36. Leo Minor, the Little Lion
37. Canes Venatici, the Hunting Dogs
38. Coma Berenices, Berenices' Hair
39. Virgo, the Virgin

The Earth travels around the Sun in one year. This makes the Sun seem to follow a particular path around the celestial sphere. The band of sky on either side of this path is called the **Zodiac**, and it passes through twelve major constellations. This means that the Sun spends about one month "in" each Zodiacal constellation.

The planets, on their own paths around the Sun, also seem to pass in front of these constellations, and so does the Moon as it orbits the Earth. Therefore, all the most important solar system objects are to be found in this band of the celestial sphere.

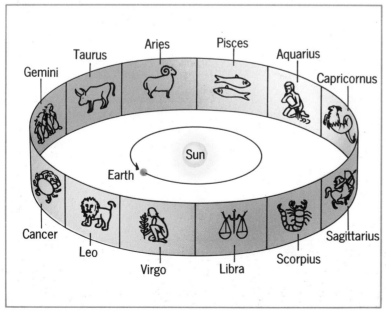

In ancient times, the positions of the Sun, Moon, and planets in the twelve constellations or "signs" of the Zodiac were thought to have some influence over us. Even today, many people believe in "astrology."

Starlight

The stars that shine out on a clear night range from bright ones seen very soon after the Sun has set, to the faintest imaginable gleams of light. The brightness of a star is called its **magnitude**. Magnitude is measured in numbers, and the smaller the magnitude number, the brighter the star.

The brightest star in the whole sky is Sirius, which is star Alpha in the constellation of Canis Major (the Greater Dog). Its magnitude is − (minus) 1.6. The faintest stars visible without binoculars are about magnitude +6 (usually written just as 6). These are each about 600 times fainter than Sirius. With binoculars, stars as faint as magnitude 9 can be made out.

Does this mean that a star of magnitude 6 is really 600 times dimmer than Sirius — that it sends out only 1/600th as much light? It certainly does not, because some stars are hundreds of times nearer to us than others are. If you look along a straight road at night, the nearest street-lights appear to be brighter than the more distant ones, even though they are all equally powerful. The same is true of the stars — the closer a star, the brighter it appears to be. Some very faint-looking stars are really much more powerful than the Sun, or than nearby Sirius. A star's real brightness is often called its luminosity, or "absolute magnitude."

One of the best-known constellations in the sky is Orion, and the brightest star is Sirius (the Dog Star), which is near Orion in the sky (shown on the left of Orion in the picture). Sirius is one of the nearest stars to the Sun, only 51 trillion miles away, or half a million times the distance from the Earth to the Sun.

Astronomers measure the huge distances between stars in light-years. A ray of light travels at a speed of 186,000 miles in one second, or 6 trillion miles in one year. Sirius is about 8.7 light-years away. The light you are now seeing from Sirius left the star almost nine years ago.

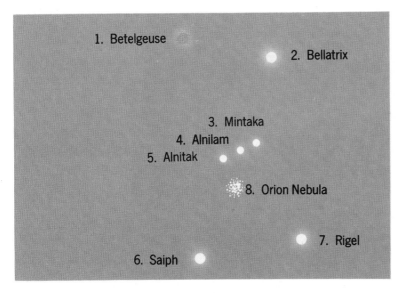

1. Betelgeuse
2. Bellatrix
3. Mintaka
4. Alnilam
5. Alnitak
8. Orion Nebula
7. Rigel
6. Saiph

The seven bright stars in Orion have all been given special names. They all appear white except for the reddish star Betelgeuse, which is a red supergiant (see page 86). The brightest star, Rigel, has a magnitude of 0, while the dimmest, Mintaka, is magnitude 2. In fact, Rigel and Mintaka are equally luminous, but Rigel appears brighter since it is closer to us.

It is not easy to measure the distance of a star, because they all look "infinitely" far away. Fortunately, astronomers have discovered ways of finding out how luminous a star really is. Knowing this, if two stars appear to be the same magnitude but one is actually more luminous than the other, then it must be farther away.

In this way we know that one of the seven bright stars in Orion, Mintaka, is 2,300 **light-years** away — twice as far away as any of the other stars in Orion and about 25 times as distant as Sirius. The solar system just happens to be in the right direction to make these scattered stars look like an attractive group in the sky.

Although we group them together, the bright stars of Orion are scattered at different distances from the Earth. The diagram below shows that Betelgeuse and Bellatrix, about 330 light-years away, are much closer to the Earth than the other five stars. The Orion Nebula, 1,300 light-years away, is also shown.

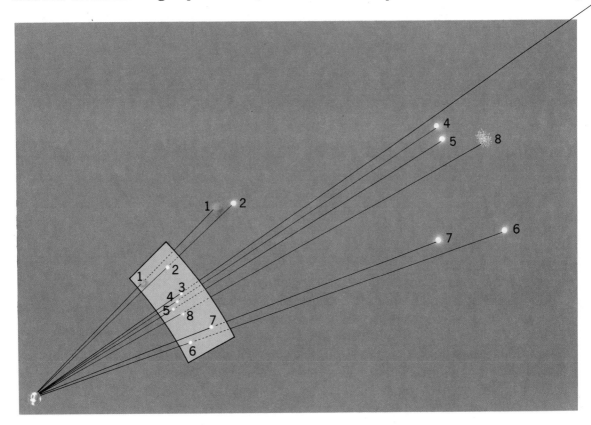

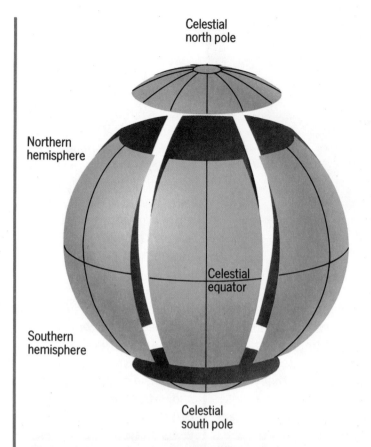

Celestial
north pole

Northern
hemisphere

Celestial
equator

Southern
hemisphere

Celestial
south pole

Many star charts divide up the celestial sphere into sections, as shown on the left. Each section maps a different part of the celestial sphere, rather like the segments of an orange.

The celestial poles show where the Earth's axis would pass through the celestial sphere. Now imagine the Earth cut through the equator into two halves, and a huge flat sheet sandwiched between them. This sheet cuts the celestial sphere in two around the celestial equator.

Stars of all kinds

The map on the opposite page shows just one section of the whole celestial sphere. Hundreds of stars can be seen on a clear night, in what appears to be a confusing mass until you have worked out where some of the brighter stars and constellations are.

Astronomers, trying to understand how stars are born, live, and die, looked for similar things and different things about the stars they observed. For example, a glance at the sky through a pair of binoculars shows that star colors range from white or blue-white through pale yellow and deep yellow to almost red. What do these colors mean? We now know the answer — that the color of a star is linked to its surface temperature. A blue-white star may be shining at about 36,000 degrees, or three times as hot as our yellowish-white Sun. A reddish star may be only half as hot as the Sun.

Astronomers also discovered that some stars are far larger than the Sun, but others are much smaller. Some spin on their axes in just a few hours. Some have other companion stars nearby, and they orbit around each other as twins. Some are still very young, and belong to a cluster of other young stars born at the same time. Some stars are dying away gently at the end of their long life, while others are pulled apart in a massive explosion.

The map opposite shows one segment of the celestial sphere, with the constellations separated by thin lines. Orion is at the center, near the celestial equator.

Some interesting special stars are marked. They are all visible with the naked eye when they have risen well above the horizon, but seen from northern countries the constellations Canis Major and Puppis never rise high in the sky.

○	Very luminous star
☼	Star like the Sun
▢	Very large and cool star
▣	Very hot star
☀	Nearby star
✕	Distant star

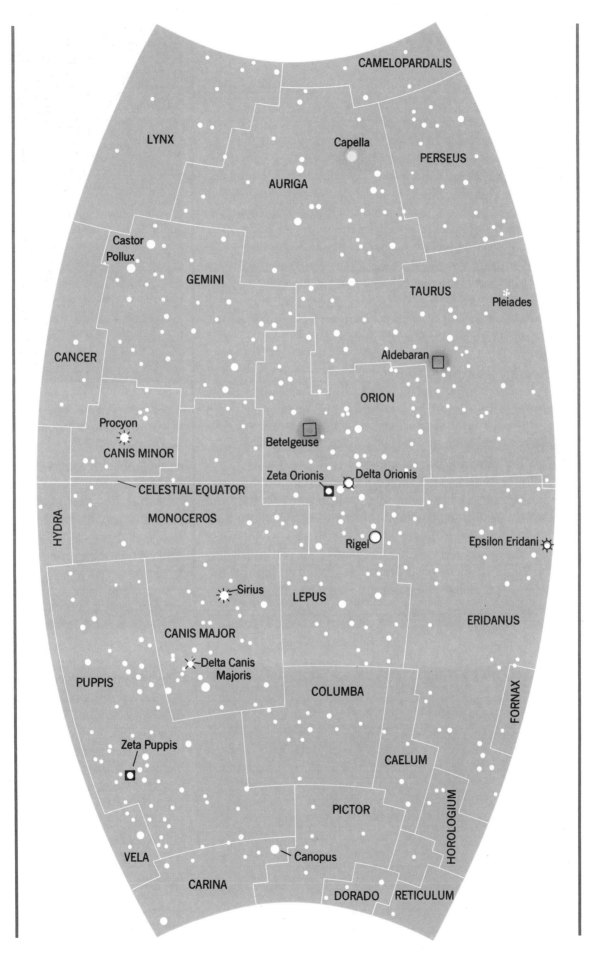

Blue giants and red dwarfs

All the stars visible in the sky were born, like the Sun, out of clouds of gas and dust. But they are not all like the Sun. Some are much hotter, and others are cooler; some are more luminous, and others are dim. This is because the stars contain different amounts of material. Some contain as much as ten or twenty Suns put together, while others have only a tenth as much as the Sun.

The more material a star contains, the hotter it becomes, because the dust and gas come together with more violence and start shining with a blaze of energy. For instance, the star Sirius has about twice as much material as the Sun — it is about five times as big as the Sun and about 5,000 degrees hotter.

Different groups of stars

Very conveniently, stars like the Sun, Sirius, and many others can be sorted into groups. The proof that there are different kinds of stars was discovered by two astronomers called Hertzsprung and Russell, who produced the diagram shown below.

If you sort stars into different colors or temperatures, from the hottest blue-white and white ones to the cool red ones, and then also divide them up according to how luminous they are, the result is clear to see — hot blue-white stars are very luminous, and cool red stars are very faint. The hottest stars, at the top left of the diagram, are called "blue giants," because they may be

The Pleiades star cluster was born perhaps 60 million years ago. The bright "Seven Sisters" are blue giants, 10,000 times more luminous than the Sun. The cluster also contains red dwarfs and stars like the Sun, but these are too dim to be made out.

Bright	36,000°F Blue-white	18,000°F White	10,800°F Yellow	8,100°F Orange	5,400°F Red
(lighthouse)	●				
(streetlamp)		●			
(desk lamp)			●		
(flashlight)				●	
(matchstick) Dim					●

The Hertzsprung-Russell diagram is a key to our understanding of the stars. The brilliant "lighthouse" stars are blue giants — large and very hot. The dim "matchstick" stars are small red dwarfs. The Sun, a yellowish "table-lamp" star, is about halfway between these extremes. If a blue giant was placed at the center of the solar system, its raging heat would melt the Earth and boil away the ice from the outermost planets.

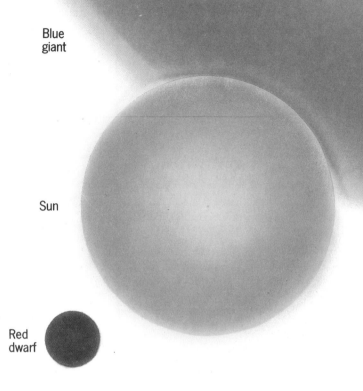

Blue
giant

Sun

Red
dwarf

twenty times the diameter of the Sun. The small dim ones, at the bottom right, are called "red dwarfs."

Giant hot stars are very rare — not more than one in a thousand. This is easy to prove, because they are so brilliant that they shine out clearly even if they are many thousands of light-years away, and not many have been discovered. They also have a very short lifetime — millions of years compared with billions of years for the Sun. This is because they use up their hydrogen supply at a tremendous rate.

Stars in the middle group, where the Sun belongs, are much more common. There are probably millions of stars like the Sun in our star city or Galaxy. But the commonest kind of star seems to be the red dwarf type. The problem is that these are too dim to make out clearly unless they are fairly close, within one or two hundred light-years of the Sun.

Looking around the region of space within 11 light-years of the Sun, ten out of the 16 known stars (including the Sun) are red dwarfs, and only two are more luminous than the Sun. There are no giant stars anywhere near as close as this. Therefore, at least half of all the stars shining in our Galaxy at the present time may be red dwarfs.

A red dwarf star may have only a tenth as much material in it as the Sun — a blue giant may have twenty times as much. But their size difference is much greater. This is because the violent energy being produced inside a star is trying to blow it apart, and only gravity holds the star together. The force of energy pouring out from the core of a hot giant star makes it swell up much more than a cooler star.

This diagram cannot show how brilliant a blue giant really is. Some giant stars send out 50,000 times as much light as the Sun.

85

Red giants and white dwarfs

The family of stars from blue giants to red dwarfs are "normal" stars in the prime of life, shining away steadily by turning their hydrogen into helium. However, there comes a time when they grow old and suffer a "fuel crisis." What is going to happen to the Sun has already happened to many other stars — they have turned first into red giants and finally into white dwarfs.

The hotter the star, the more quickly its core of "dead" helium swells. The force of its heat blasts the surface of the star outward in a glowing shell. This shell cools down to red-heat, since it is now much farther away from the hot core that heats it. It may even puff in and out.

A dying star

Our Sun may one day grow as large as the orbit of Venus, but the red star Betelgeuse, in Orion, is already so huge that the orbit of the Earth could fit inside it. If you had visited the Earth when the first ape-men walked the planet, Betelgeuse would probably have looked white — it was then a fiercely hot giant star.

Come back to Earth in a few more million years, and you will look in vain for Betelgeuse unless you have a powerful telescope. In its place will be a dim white dwarf just one-millionth of its present brightness. White dwarfs are so dim that very few people have ever seen one. For most stars, they mark the beginning of the end.

A red supergiant is so enormous that it seems impossible for it to end up as a tiny white dwarf. But its hydrogen gas is spread very thinly. A sample of the outer layers of Betelgeuse the size of the Earth would weigh as much as a small bag of potatoes.

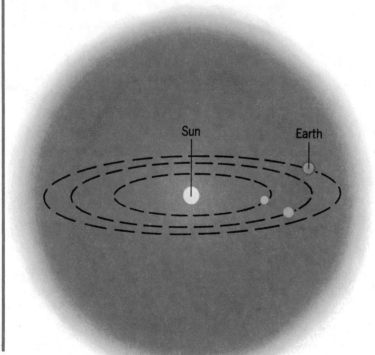

Sun

Earth

This diagram shows the size of the red supergiant star Betelgeuse compared with the Earth's orbit. Before it began to swell up it probably measured ten times the width of the Sun. Now it is at least 200 times the width.

The center of a sunspot, which appears so dark compared with the Sun's photosphere, is actually hotter and brighter than the surface of Betelgeuse! Betelgeuse shines so strongly only because it has a huge surface sending out light.

Sun

Red
supergiant

White dwarf

Passing through the red giant and white dwarf stages is the "quiet" way for a star to die — and most stars, apart from the hottest blue giants, do end their lives quietly. During the red giant stage about a third of all their hydrogen and helium atoms leak back into space. Eventually, these atoms will go to form new gas and dust clouds that may give birth to new stars, so that the process begins all over again.

On the next page, we shall look at the more violent ending of a different type of star — the supernova.

This version of the Hertzsprung-Russell diagram shows how red giants and white dwarfs are completely different from other stars. A white dwarf star will cool down and change color to yellow and red, and finally will die to blackness. Astronomers call these dying star embers "brown dwarfs" and "black dwarfs." A black dwarf would be invisible unless a spacecraft happened to pass nearby and see its outline against other stars.

Bright	36,000°F Blue-white	18,000°F White	10,800°F Yellow	8,100°F Orange	5,400°F Red
Dim					

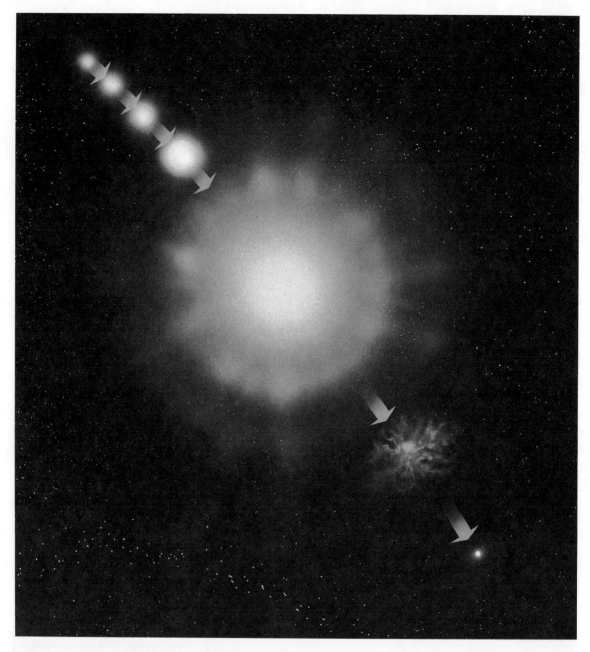

Exploding stars

Not every star ends "peacefully" as a puffing red giant and a smoldering white dwarf. The most massive and hottest stars, known as blue or white supergiants, may sometimes destroy themselves in the most violent way possible — by blowing up as a supernova.

A star is like a nuclear bomb, and only the force of its gravity stops it from blowing apart. The more material a star contains, the more its force of gravity tries to pull all its material into the center. When a really massive star uses up all its fuel, it collapses. The temperature at its center jumps to about 5 billion degrees, and the result is a supernova explosion.

A supernova explosion is set off in seconds when a supergiant star collapses. For a week or two, the disaster gives off as much light as a whole galaxy of stars. After it dies down all that is left is a gas shell, a nebula, with a tiny "neutron star" less than 30 miles across at the center — the star's crushed core. In time the nebula fades away, leaving just the dim neutron star.

A hydrogen atom is the simplest one of all, because it contains a single electron orbiting around a single proton. The electron travels so fast in so many directions around the proton that the atom would look like a round ball, if anyone could manage to see one.

But most of an atom is empty space. The lower picture gives a better idea of this. If the proton at its center was the size of a pea, the electron whizzing around it would be about 700 feet away.

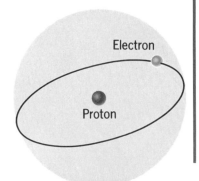

The collapse of a star

All that may be left after a supernova explosion is a tiny **neutron star** — one of the strangest objects in the universe. A neutron star is totally solid matter — a trillion times heavier than lead. A matchbox-sized sample of white dwarf material would weigh several tons, but a pinhead piece of a neutron star would weigh as much as a large building!

It is hard to imagine, but even the most solid object around you is almost all empty space. Everything is made up of atoms, but atoms are not solid. For example, a hydrogen atom, which is the commonest of all, has a solid particle (a **proton**) at the center, and a much smaller particle (an electron) whirling around it in an orbit millions of times every second. Atoms are too small to see, but if you made a scale model of a hydrogen atom using a pea to represent the proton, the orbit of the electron would have to be more than 400 yards across. The enormous space inside this orbit is empty except for the pea-sized proton.

In a white dwarf, the atoms of hydrogen and helium are squashed together until they are touching each other. In the center of an exploding supernova, however, the atoms are crushed so hard that the actual protons and electrons are themselves squashed together, forming a different type of atomic particle called a **neutron**. The result is the most solid matter possible in the universe — a neutron star.

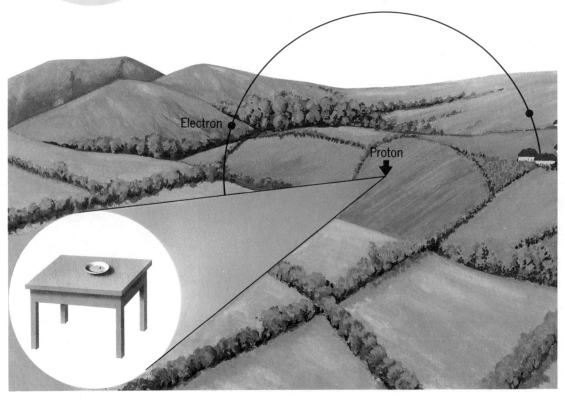

89

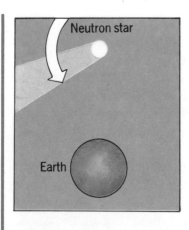

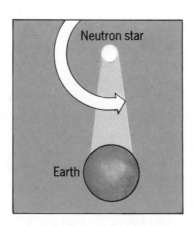

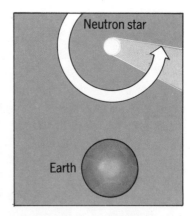

Signals from the stars

Twenty years ago, a small group of astronomers working at Cambridge, in England, made a discovery. Their radio telescope was picking up a regular "pip" every second, keeping time as accurately as their best clock. Were they picking up intelligent signals from space? Instead, they discovered that the signals came from a spinning neutron star, and they called it a "pulsar."

Soon after, a pulsar was discovered at the center of the most famous supernova shell in the sky — the Crab Nebula. This supernova was seen and recorded by Chinese astronomers in the year 1054. The neutron star, the remains of the massive exploding star, is a dim speck inside the nebula, spinning 30 times a second. As it spins, it sends out a lighthouse-beam of radio waves and light, which passes across the Earth.

The strong magnetic field of a spinning neutron star forces its energy waves into a narrow beam. Each "sweep" of the beam over Earth can be picked up by radio, or photographed. Over millions of years, pulsars slow down and this "lighthouse" effect ends.

The Crab Nebula is shown below, with the position of its pulsar marked by the box. The pulsar looks like a small star.

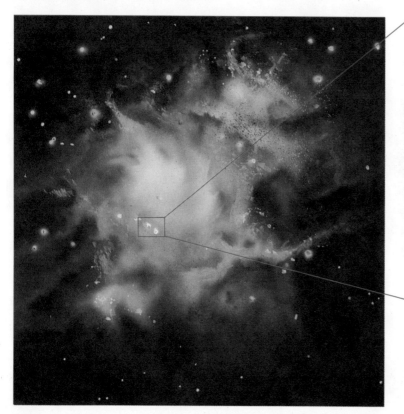

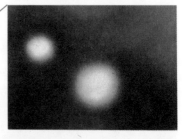

The pulsar is the bottom star in the picture above. When the beam swings away from the Earth, the pulsar seems to vanish.

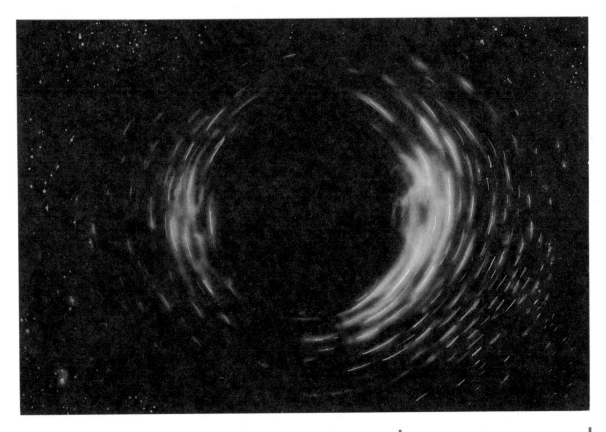

The final stage

Is a neutron star the final stage of a supernova? Well, no — there may be one more stage, the most amazing of all. It can completely disappear.

Every object in the universe has its own force of gravity. The Earth's gravity pulls everything down on to its surface. If the Earth were somehow squeezed down to half its size, its gravity would feel so strong that you could only crawl around. If it collapsed down to the size of a neutron star, your bones and body would be crushed flat by the force.

When a star collapses into a neutron star, even **light waves** can find it difficult to escape. The gravity of a small neutron star, like the pulsar inside the Crab Nebula, is not strong enough to hold its light waves back, but a larger one would be. It could be shining brightly, but no light or radio waves could ever escape. It would be completely "black" — a **black hole**.

Like the Tardis time machine in *Dr. Who*, a black hole turns space inside out. From the outside, it might appear a round black object only a few miles across. But if you were inside it, it would seem as big as a universe. You could not see anything outside it, but you could not find its "edge," either!

Astronomers have not yet seen a black hole itself, but they have found stars that could have an invisible black hole nearby. There could be a huge black hole at the center of our Milky Way Galaxy.

If you were close to a black hole, it might appear like this — a round black disk with a pattern of bright lights around the edge. The light comes from distant stars behind the black hole, but it has been "bent" and distorted by the fierce gravity around the hole — rather like the flow of water around a pebble in a stream.

A star passing near a black hole may be pulled slightly out of its path by the black hole's gravity. But unless it is heading straight for the hole, it will pass on its way as if nothing had happened. Black holes do not "pull" objects inside them. If they did, then by this time they would have swallowed just about everything in sight!

91

Twin stars

About a quarter of all the stars studied by astronomers are "twins," two stars orbiting around each other. These are called "binary stars." For example, the bright star Sirius has a companion — a dim white dwarf. These two stars are about as far apart as the Sun and Uranus, and take 50 years to go around each other once.

Binary stars must have been born together inside the same cloud, because the chances of one star "capturing" another passing star are tiny — single stars are too far apart in space.

Some binary stars are beautiful to look at through a telescope — a few can even be seen using binoculars. They are also very important, because although they are formed at the same time, they are often completely different in color and brightness. This discovery helped astronomers to realize that some kinds of stars grow older faster than others.

We are sure that the present dim companion of Sirius was once the brighter and hotter star of the two. But it has already passed through its red giant stage and turned into a faint white dwarf, while Sirius, a cooler star, shines steadily on. Many millions of years ago, during that red-giant stage of its companion, someone looking up at the sky would have seen a star like Betelgeuse shining where Sirius shines today.

If you were on a "lost planet" traveling through space, you might pass near a binary star looking like this. A bright white star shines nearby, and much farther off a huge red giant casts an orange-red glow over the landscape. As the planet travels on its way, these two suns will seem to move apart, or swing closer together, casting confusing shadows.

It is very unlikely that any planet could stay in orbit around a binary star. The different gravities of the two stars would keep changing the planet's orbit, until finally it would fly off into space to travel endlessly among the stars.

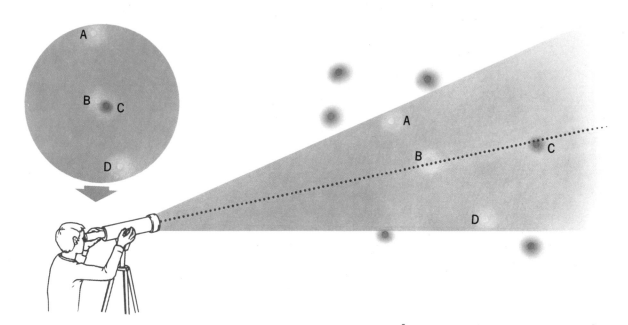

The two stars in a binary pair seem to move around each other as if they were the weights on a spinning dumbbell. In fact, each one is traveling around on its own separate orbit. Astronomers, using powerful telescopes, can measure their slow turning.

Some star systems contain four stars — two binary pairs, each revolving around the other pair. The bright star Castor (Alpha in the constellation of Gemini, the Twins), contains three binary pairs revolving around each other, so that what looks like a single star to us on Earth is really six stars.

From a distance, two trees may seem to be side by side, when one is really several fields nearer than the other. Some stars show the same effect; they look close together through a telescope, but really they are just in the same "line of sight." These are known as optical double stars.

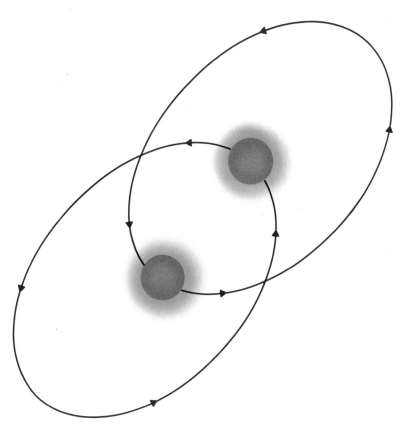

The diagram on the left shows how two members of a binary system may orbit each other. Some pairs of stars keep about the same distance apart all the time, while other pairs pass close to each other and then swing far apart. Some binary stars are so close together that they touch each other. Others are much farther apart than the Sun and Pluto, and a single orbit takes thousands of years.

About 70,000 binary stars and optical double stars have been observed, but there are certainly many more waiting to be found.

Changing stars

A star like the Sun has been shining steadily for billions of years. Even a small change in its heat and light would mean the end of life on the Earth, so we can be sure that it has not changed much in all that time. But stars do change in brightness, sometimes in a matter of hours, or over years. These are known as **variable stars**.

Some of these variable stars are binaries. When one star passes in front of its companion, the light from the companion is cut off from our view. From the Earth, it seems as if a single star fades away and then brightens again. These are called "eclipsing binaries," and they change so regularly that astronomers can forecast to the minute when they will be bright or faint for years ahead.

Other stars really do change the amount of light they give out. Some of them are going through the difficult stage of turning from ordinary stars into red giants. Their outer layers are swelling up and shrinking down again like a balloon, and as they change in size they also change in brightness. This type of star is found in a famous group of variable stars called **Cepheids** — named after a star in the constellation Cepheus. Most of them take several days to puff up and down once.

Once a star becomes a red giant it is likely to keep on being variable, but it does not change in brightness very much. Betelgeuse, for example, can seem different from one year to another, but you would have to measure its magnitude very accurately to notice the change.

A Cepheid variable star swells and shrinks. We cannot see the change in its size from Earth, but we do see a change in its brightness.

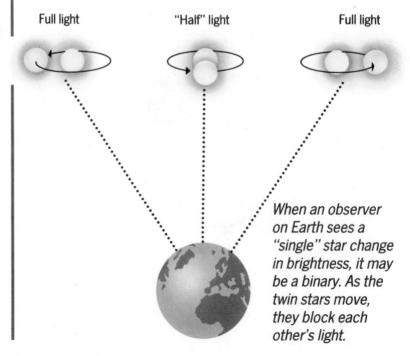

Full light   "Half" light   Full light

When an observer on Earth sees a "single" star change in brightness, it may be a binary. As the twin stars move, they block each other's light.

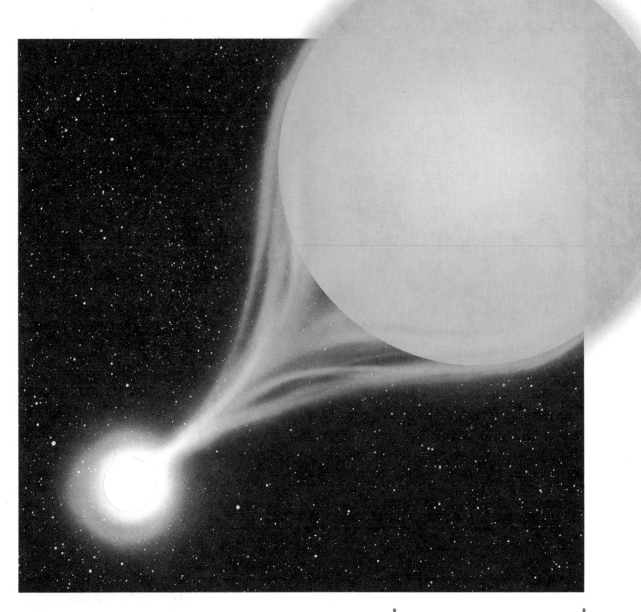

Going nova

Some variable stars take astronomers by surprise. These are the "novas." A **nova** is a binary star. The two stars are very close together, and one of them is a dim but very hot white dwarf. Its gravity pulls clouds of hydrogen away from the larger and cooler star, and when the hydrogen reaches the dwarf's hot surface it explodes.

The white dwarf may take hundreds of years to collect enough hydrogen for an explosion. Then, one night, an astronomer watching the sky notices a "new" star not marked on a map, and he or she knows that a nova has erupted. The explosion does not last long — after less than a week it is usually beginning to die down again.

Every year, one or two novas are close enough to the Sun to be seen with small telescopes or even binoculars. The brightest nova for many years shone out in the constellation of Cygnus (the Swan) in 1975, and was easy to see with the naked eye. Another nova may blaze up in the sky at any time.

This is what a nova explosion might look like. The burst of light from the cloud around the white dwarf makes the whole binary star suddenly appear between 10,000 and a million times brighter than normal.

A supernova destroys itself, but the exploding star in a nova system starts building up "fuel" for another explosion all over again. Astronomers have seen some novas explode several times, with twenty or thirty years between outbursts.

An imaginary rocky world passes near a globular cluster. Countless stars swarm here, as they have done since they were born together perhaps 12 billion years ago. This cluster would be about three times as old as the solar system, and probably two-thirds as old as the universe.

When a globular cluster was young it contained all sorts of stars, including stars like the Sun, perhaps with planets orbiting around them. Most of these stars have gone through their lives and are now white dwarfs, or even black dwarfs. But there are still enough red giants shining to make a dazzling display.

Star clusters

Star clusters are among the most beautiful sights in the sky. Amateur astronomers enjoy "showing off" some of the brightest ones to their friends. But they are also very important. All stars were born in clusters, and many still belong to them.

The biggest kinds of clusters are called "globulars." These can contain up to half a million stars in the same amount of space that holds just a few hundred stars near the Earth. It is a pity that they are all so many thousands of light-years away from the Sun. Photographs can only give us the faintest hint of what a swarm of half a million stars must look like.

All globular clusters were formed a long time ago — long before the Sun was born. In their youth they had many brilliant white stars. Many of these have aged into white dwarfs too dim to see. The stars that are visible now are all old red giants.

The powerful gravity of a globular cluster holds its stars tightly together. But it is possible that the clusters themselves move around, like swarms of bees. They may even escape from the galaxy where they were born, and drift off into the dark vastness of space toward other far distant galaxies.

Another kind of cluster is the "open" cluster. It may only contain a few hundred stars, and it will not be as old. Open clusters are still being formed and all kinds of stars can be found inside them.

Open clusters

The Sun was probably formed inside an "open" cluster, together with a few hundred other stars. Open clusters are the birthplaces of stars, and young clusters can be seen shining inside the clouds of gas and dust that produced them. Since these stars are much farther apart than the ones inside a globular cluster, they drift apart rather easily. There are not many old open clusters left in one piece.

Open clusters are interesting because they contain all kinds of stars. You will find brilliant blue giants, stars like the Sun, and red dwarfs in a newly formed cluster, like

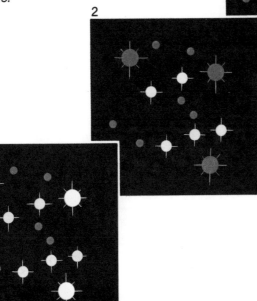

The stars found in an open cluster change over about 10 billion years.

1. At first, there are bright white stars, medium-yellow stars like the Sun, and dim red dwarfs.

2. The bright white stars quickly become red giants.
3. These then fade out as white dwarfs. By this time, the yellow stars have also become red giants.
4. Finally, these too turn into white dwarfs. But the dim red dwarfs just shine on, with hardly any change. They will be the last stars to die away.

the famous Pleiades or Seven Sisters in the constellation Taurus (the Bull). An older open cluster, like the Hyades — also in Taurus — has no blue giants left, but plenty of red giants. The blue giants burned themselves out long ago. So by seeing which kinds of stars are inside a cluster, an astronomer can decide how young or old it is.

Open clusters will go on being formed as long as there is gas and dust in a galaxy to produce stars. When the "fuel" runs out, star-making will end. But our own Galaxy looks healthy for many billions of years yet, and new clusters will be giving birth to new stars even when the Sun has sunk to a glowing speck.

Clouds in space

Not even half the material that makes up the universe is in the stars. A lot of it exists as single invisible atoms of hydrogen spread through space, both between the galaxies and inside them. But a great deal can also be seen as enormous clouds of hydrogen and tiny solid particles of dust. Some of these clouds are dark, while others are bright, and some are dark with glowing patches. They are all known as nebulas.

A single nebula can be a thousand light-years across, which is big enough to hold a trillion solar systems. If you are in the countryside on a clear dark night and look up at the Milky Way, which is the part of our own Galaxy that we can see, you will notice dark patches blocking out some of the starlight. These are huge black nebulas.

A nebula is as dark and cold as anything can be — about 450 degrees below zero — until it starts to shrink and collapse to form hot young stars. Then, once a few stars begin to shine, parts of it light up. The dust in a nebula reflects starlight, just as clouds over the Earth can shine in sunlight. However, nebular dust does not shine very strongly. What really lights up is the gas. This shines because of the energy waves coming from the young stars, which make the gas atoms glow. It is the same effect that switches on an aurora, as described on page 45.

This photograph of the Horsehead Nebula in Orion shows just a small part of the famous Orion Nebula. This is a fairly small nebula, only 15 light-years across. It is important because it is near to Earth, and can be seen with the naked eye.

The bright part is shining because of newborn stars in the center of the nebula. Their heat and light do not reach other parts, which remain dark. The dark horsehead-shaped cloud is a fountain of cool gas and dust that stands out against the bright gas behind. Stars are still being formed in the Orion Nebula.

The photograph on the right is the Trifid Nebula. It is in the constellation Sagittarius (the Archer), and appears much fainter than the Orion Nebula because it is about five times farther away from the Sun. Its distance is about 6,000 light-years, so that the light reaching us now began its journey before the Egyptian pyramids were built.

It is also slightly larger than the Orion Nebula, measuring about 25 light-years across. Strands of dark nebulas lie in front of the bright gas where stars are forming.

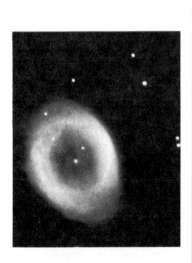

The planetary nebula known as the Ring Nebula, in the constellation of Lyra (the Lyre), can be seen with a telescope. It is about 1,400 light-years away and about half a light-year across — 500 times the diameter of Pluto's orbit.

"Left-over" stars

There is another kind of nebula in space. This sort does not make stars — it is made by them instead. They are called "planetary nebulas," because when seen through a telescope, some of them look round and sharp, like a dim planet. The most famous planetary nebula is the Crab Nebula, which is shown on page 90 and is the wreck of a supernova that was seen nine hundred years ago.

All the 92 different elements in the universe, such as hydrogen, oxygen, carbon, and iron, are different only because their atoms are made up of different numbers of protons and electrons. Inside a very hot star, these atomic particles are being jumbled up and rearranged the whole time. As well as turning hydrogen atoms into helium atoms, the star is also "creating" other elements. When the star explodes, these elements are thrown out into space in a planetary nebula. Eventually the planetary nebula fades away and the atoms drift into other nebulas, where they may give birth to other stars — and solar systems. It is possible that the carbon atoms in your body, or those making up this page, were once scattered into space as part of a planetary nebula.

99

Other solar systems

Are there other planets like the Earth? We may never know for certain, because even the nearest star is so far away that our biggest telescopes would have no hope of making out a planet like Earth, or even a giant planet like Jupiter, at such a distance.

Many astronomers once believed that the planets were formed by another wandering star passing near the Sun and pulling out from it a cloud of gas and dust, which turned into the planets. If this was what happened solar systems would be very rare, because stars hardly ever pass close by each other. But the modern idea is that planets are likely to form around many stars quite naturally. And even if only one in a hundred stars produces planets, there must be a billion other solar systems in our Galaxy alone.

Although planets belonging to other stars may never be seen, it may be possible to find them by discovering if a star shows a slight "wobble" in its position. For instance, Jupiter's gravity makes the Sun move from side to side by over a half a million miles as it slowly circles in its orbit. Some astronomers suspect that a few nearby stars are steadily shifting from side to side because an invisible giant planet is tugging at them.

The picture on the right shows an imaginary solar system. There could be many solar systems in the universe completely different from our own. Some might contain just one huge planet, even bigger than Jupiter; others might be nothing but asteroid-sized bodies, or even comets.

It is possible that one of the Voyager space probes may drift into such a solar system, many thousands of years after it has left our own. By this time, however, the space probe will be just a piece of ancient wreckage.

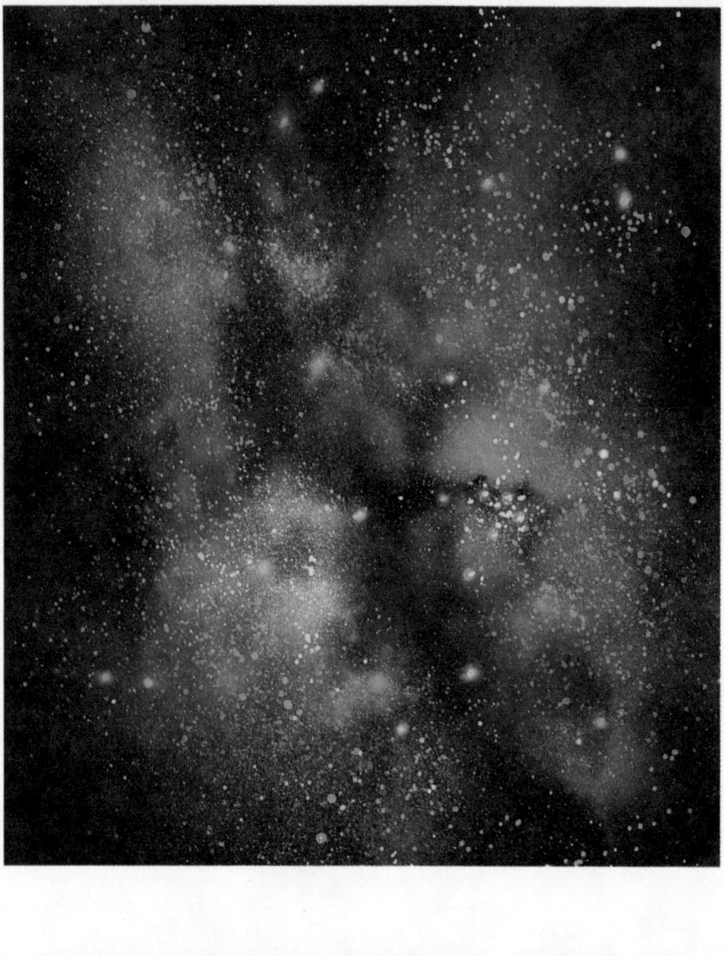

Just one small part of our own Galaxy, with its star clouds and nebulas, contains millions of stars. Among them there must surely be countless thousands of stars with one or more planets orbiting around them.

Some of these planets could belong to stars like the Sun, and even have an atmosphere and seas like the Earth. But they are all so far away that we can never hope to see any of these planets from Earth.

The diagram below shows how the gravitational pull of a giant planet could make a star wobble in its path, even though the planet itself is too dim to be seen. Some astronomers believe that the star Epsilon in the constellation Eridanus (see page 83) moves like this, but the wobble, if any, is so tiny that no one can be sure.

Both of the Voyager space probes are heading out of the solar system and may one day drift as derelict wrecks into strange solar systems. Perhaps they will pass rocky and icy planets like the ones they left behind. Or they may find completely different types of worlds. There could be pairs of planets making identical twins, or planets spinning so fast that they are throwing off showers of material like a hose, or misty planets like huge comet heads.

It is even possible that a true comet, a wanderer from our own solar system, would arrive with the probes to display its tail alongside the nearby star.

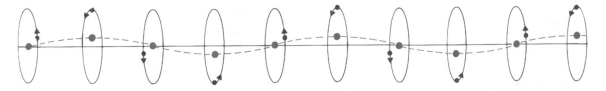

On its own, a star travels steadily through space.

But the pull of an orbiting planet will make it "wobble" as it moves along.

6. Discovering the Universe

The galaxies of space

Stars and nebulas do not wander freely through space. They are collected together in vast groups called galaxies. A galaxy like our own Milky Way Galaxy contains about a hundred billion stars, as well as nebulas. Some other galaxies are much larger than this.

The Milky Way Galaxy is shaped like a spiral. From Earth, astronomers have seen millions of spiral galaxies, and have taken beautiful photographs of those nearest to us. Their centers contain old red giant stars, while the arms are a mixture of nebulas, old stars and young stars, as well as star clusters. Spiral galaxies are turning around, but so slowly that you could not see any movement even if you watched for hundreds of years.

The Whirlpool Galaxy lies 14 million light-years away. It is smaller than our own Milky Way Galaxy, but there is a companion galaxy close by, and the two are connected by very faint wisps of gas and dust. This is a beautiful example of a spiral galaxy, with red giants (old stars) near the center. Stars of mixed ages, some young, some old, make up the arms of the galaxy.

Most elliptical galaxies, like the one shown at the top of the page, have a smooth shape. They contain some of the oldest stars in the universe. This one is a "satellite" of the Andromeda Galaxy.

Below it is an irregular galaxy in Ursa Major. It is 8.5 million light-years away. Some kind of violent explosion seems to be happening inside it — perhaps it is colliding with a huge cloud of gas.

Elliptical galaxies

Other galaxies are like the center of a spiral galaxy but without any arms. These are called "elliptical" galaxies because of their shape, and they include the largest and the smallest galaxies known. "Giant" elliptical galaxies may contain ten times as many stars as our own Galaxy, but "dwarf" ellipticals have no more stars than a large globular cluster. Some of the most far-off galaxies found by astronomers are of the giant elliptical type, but the dwarf ones are so dim that even the nearest ones are too faint to see properly.

Elliptical galaxies are not just different from spirals in the way they look — they are different inside, too. There seem to be practically no nebulas inside an elliptical galaxy. Since new stars are formed from nebulas this means that elliptical galaxies have no new stars, and their "populations" of stars are slowly dying of old age. In fact, most elliptical galaxies are made up of cool red giant stars quietly glowing their way toward the white dwarf stage.

Irregular galaxies

The third type of galaxy is known as the "irregular" type. These galaxies do not have any particular shape, and they are all smaller than the Milky Way. Unlike elliptical galaxies, the stars inside them are mostly young, with only a few old red giants. There is plenty of hydrogen gas available to form new stars, so irregular galaxies may end up as the longest-living galaxies in the universe, producing more and more stars for thousands of years after the stars in the elliptical and spiral galaxies have ceased to shine.

103

The Milky Way Galaxy

To be able to see the size and layout of a town, you must go high up into the sky to see the whole area spread out below. Otherwise, all you can see is a group of nearby buildings. It is the same with our view of our own Galaxy — the patchy, star-speckled band of light that we call the Milky Way is the only view we have. It is like holding a town map level with your eyes, and only seeing a thin strip. If you could put it down on a table, the whole plan of the town could be seen at a glance.

This strip of light in the sky, the Milky Way, is our edge-on view of the nearer arms of the spiral. We can easily see the closest and brightest stars in the skies above Earth, but the rest of the arms, and the center of the Galaxy, are always hidden behind these closer stars and nebulas. The dark patches in the Milky Way are caused by clouds of dust blocking out the stars beyond.

The Milky Way, seen in the constellations Scorpius and Sagittarius (the Scorpion and the Archer). To see the Milky Way like this, you need to be in southern Europe or the southern United States. But the best view of all is seen from the Earth's southern hemisphere.

Huge dark nebulas make the Milky Way appear uneven in brightness. The blazing center of the Galaxy is completely hidden by these dusty clouds.

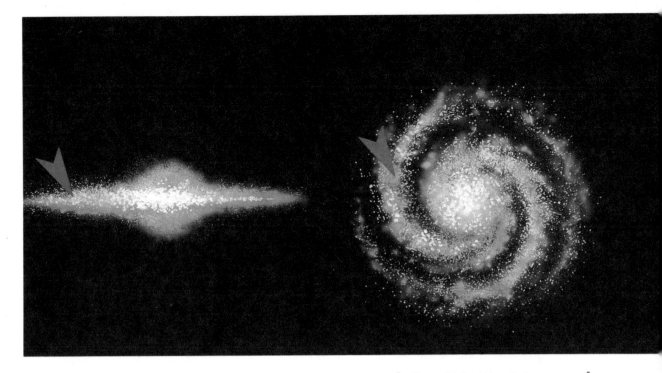

The shape of the Galaxy

Once astronomers discovered that other galaxies in the universe are spiral, it helped them to understand the shape of the Milky Way Galaxy. Even though we cannot see our whole Galaxy, it is possible to have a reasonable idea of what it would look like if it was seen by observers in another nearby galaxy.

The Galaxy measures about 100,000 light-years across. To get some idea of its vast size, you could imagine that the distance between the Earth and the Sun is about 3 inches. On this scale, the diameter of the Galaxy would be equal to the true distance between the Earth and the Moon.

Our place in the Galaxy

Our Sun is about 30,000 light-years from the Galactic center, and the central mass of old red giants forming the nucleus is about 20,000 light-years across. There are also several hundred globular clusters scattered about the nucleus. This means that they are all thousands of light-years away from the Sun, which explains why most of them are only dim shapes to us, even though each one contains up to a million stars.

The Sun lies near the edge of one of the Galactic arms, and it is being carried around the center of the Galaxy, with all the other nearby stars, once every 220 million years. The arms contain dust clouds, gas clouds, young and old star clusters, and young and old stars. There are almost certainly millions of other stars like the Sun, with planets orbiting them, elsewhere in the arms of the Milky Way Galaxy.

If our Milky Way Galaxy could be seen from far out in space, it would appear something like the two views shown here. Edge-on, the Galaxy looks like a flat disk with a swollen middle — the nucleus. From above, it looks like a whirlpool of stars. The position of our Sun, and therefore our solar system, is marked in both views by the red arrow.

The stars in the nucleus date back to the early days of the Galaxy — the ones still shining are red giants.

The spiral arms are very different, with many middle-aged stars like the Sun, as well as young stars that have been recently formed inside the Galaxy's nebulas.

This photograph of a nearby spiral galaxy gives us a good idea of what our own Galaxy must look like. The arms of this galaxy are more "open" than the arms of our own star system, however, and the central nucleus is smaller.

The center of the Galaxy

The true center of the Milky Way Galaxy is a mystery. Vast clouds of dust block it from sight, otherwise it would shine as brightly as the Full Moon. However, using radio telescopes to pick up radio waves, which can pass through the dust clouds, astronomers have discovered a huge shell of gas clouds within 1,000 light-years of the Galaxy's center, flying outward at a speed of more than 60 miles per second!

This explosion of gas shows that there must be a tremendous power source at the very center of the Galaxy. One explanation is that a huge black hole is giving out powerful energy waves as material falls into it.

The view below shows how the Milky Way might appear in the night sky if the solar system was a few hundred light-years above the Galaxy's arms. No dust clouds hide the blazing nucleus, but there would be no one to see it — the fierce energy waves from the center would have prevented any life from developing on Earth.

The spiral arms

Most of the stars we can see lie within a few hundred light-years of the Sun, in the same spiral arm or another arm nearby. But these are the brighter stars — the dimmer ones are too faint to be seen without a telescope, even though they are among the Sun's nearest neighbors. In fact, the commonest stars near the Sun (and perhaps throughout the arms of the Galaxy) are red dwarfs, so dim that a thousand collected together would not shine as brightly as our own star.

Our Galaxy must be at least 12 billion years old, because that seems to be the age of the oldest stars we can see. This means that the Sun and the other stars in the spiral arms must have traveled many times around the center of the Galaxy. If this is so, it seems strange that the arms have not wound up into a tight ball. This could be because stars and nebulas do not stay in the arms for all time, but pass through them, like water through waves, in the course of many millions of years.

On the move

At the present time, the Sun appears to be near the inner edge of one of the spiral arms. If the "wave" theory is right, millions of years into the future could find the solar system in more crowded star regions, or else passing through the lonely wastes between the arms. Space between the arms is less "dusty," and it is even possible that direct energy waves from the brilliant Galactic center might shine upon the planets for a time. This could, in turn, have an effect upon life on the Earth. Perhaps a previous trip between the arms has already affected our planet in the past?

On the Earth, only half the sky can be seen at any one time — the other half is below the horizon. By patiently photographing the whole of the Milky Way, astronomer Knut Lundmark was able to piece together an edge-on view of the complete Galaxy as seen from the Earth.

The middle of the picture shows the view toward the center of the Galaxy, but the brilliant nucleus is blocked by dust — most of the stars and nebulas shown here are in the spiral arms.

The "ends" of the picture are much dimmer. This is the view of the Milky Way arms beyond the Sun's position, looking out toward intergalactic space.

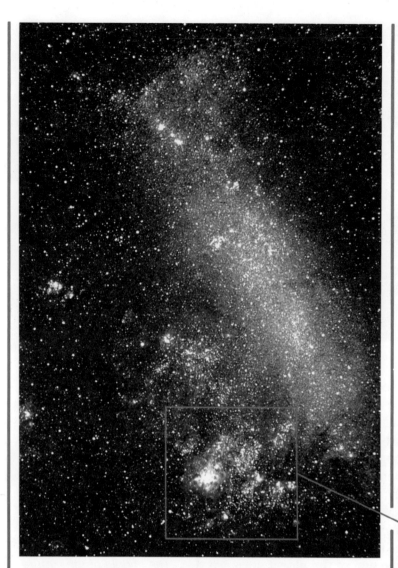

The two Magellanic Clouds are about 200,000 light-years away. All the single stars shown spread across this photograph of the Large Cloud are nearby stars in our own Galaxy, hundreds or thousands of times closer than the Cloud itself.

You can see that there are hardly any dark nebulas present in this galaxy. Dark nebulas contain dust, and dust comes from old exploding stars — the Cloud has not yet produced enough stars for much dust to have collected.

Galactic neighbors

Stars are born in clusters, and galaxies also exist in groups. Our Galaxy belongs to what we call the **Local Group** — a collection of about 30 galaxies. The Milky Way Galaxy also has two small galaxies, called the Magellanic Clouds, which seem to be in orbit around it, like satellites. These can be seen as dim patches of light, from the Earth's southern hemisphere.

The Magellanic Clouds are irregular galaxies, and astronomers using big telescopes have such a good view of them that they are probably the best-known galaxies in the universe. Most of the stars that can be seen in the Magellanic Clouds are young hot giants, and there are many nebulas giving birth to new stars, but there are few red giants. In February 1987, a star in the Large Magellanic Cloud exploded as a supernova — the nearest and brightest seen from Earth since the one observed in our own Galaxy in 1604.

In February 1987, a super-nova was discovered in the Large Cloud, in the area shown by the box in the photograph on the left. This photograph was taken before the supernova exploded. The small photograph above shows the same area, but with the new supernova appearing as an intense patch of light (inside the circle).

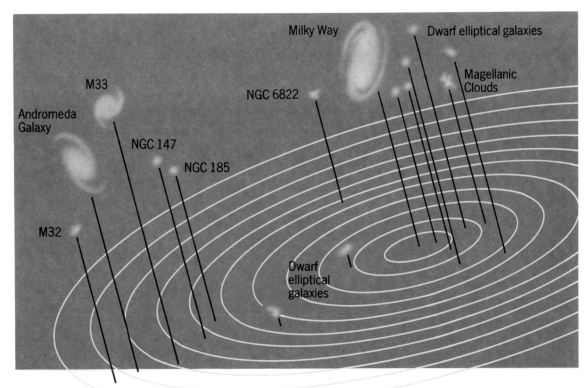

This illustration is of a dwarf elliptical galaxy, 800,000 light-years away. It is one of the smallest and dimmest known — you can just see the pinkish hazy patch of light far beyond the stars in our own Galaxy. It contains only a ten-thousandth as many stars as our own Galaxy, none of them very luminous. There may once have been some brilliant stars here, but they died away long ago.

Only three members of the Local Group are spiral galaxies. The largest of these is the **Andromeda Galaxy**, which can also be seen with the naked eye as a hazy patch. The rest are dwarf elliptical and irregular galaxies, which appear extremely faint and unspectacular, even though they are so close. Dwarf ellipticals are probably the commonest type of galaxy in the universe, but only the nearest ones can be made out, as they are even fainter than a single, very bright giant star!

There are almost certainly other members of the Local Group, but the dust clouds in our own Galaxy block huge areas of space from view, and even a large nearby galaxy could remain hidden from astronomers' telescopes.

The diagram of the Local Group below shows the galaxies so far discovered at their correct distances apart, although their sizes are not to scale. The Milky Way Galaxy and the Andromeda Galaxy are by far the largest members of the group. There is another smaller spiral galaxy, but the other galaxies are all elliptical dwarfs.

Milky Way

Dwarf elliptical galaxies

M33

Magellanic Clouds

NGC 6822

Andromeda Galaxy

NGC 147

NGC 185

M32

Dwarf elliptical galaxies

The Andromeda Galaxy

Just over two million light-years away, the Andromeda Galaxy is the most distant object you can see without a telescope. The light now reaching the Earth from this galaxy began its journey long before recognizable human beings walked on our planet.

A pair of binoculars will show you an elliptical haze with a bright center, but long-exposure photographs taken with large telescopes are necessary to make out even the brightest supergiant stars. It is so far away that a star only as bright as the Sun would be completely invisible. What stand out are the patches of bright nebulas and the vast swirls of dark nebulas in the spiral arms, as well as the huge swarm of red giants around its center. There are also two "satellites." These are dwarf elliptical galaxies.

The Andromeda Galaxy is about one and a half times the diameter of the Milky Way Galaxy, and contains perhaps 400 billion stars. Unfortunately, its position in space means that our view is almost edge-on, and we cannot see the spiral arms very well.

This photograph shows the Andromeda spiral galaxy and its two companion elliptical galaxies, seen through stars of the Milky Way Galaxy. What look like bright stars in the Andromeda Galaxy are really clusters, or brilliant nebulas, in the spiral arms.

Most of the light reaching us comes from the red giant stars in the nucleus. These are hundreds of times closer together than the stars near our Sun, which means that "night" would be as bright as "day" to a planet orbiting around one of them. By comparison with the nucleus the arms are dim, cool, and empty.

Discovering the distance

Measuring the distance to the Andromeda Galaxy has been a difficult problem. More than a hundred years ago, before good photographs were available, it was believed to be a nearby star giving birth to planets! But even when it was discovered to be a galaxy of stars, there was no way of measuring the distance until astronomers could identify a star inside it whose real brightness (absolute magnitude) was known. The distance of the star, and therefore of the galaxy, could then be worked out by deciding how far away the star must be to appear as bright as it did.

This could not be done until the 100-inch telescope was built on Mount Wilson, in California, in 1917. This was powerful enough to photograph some of the most luminous giant stars in the Andromeda Galaxy, and gave astronomers the first clue to the enormous distances between galaxies in space.

When most of the lights of nearby Los Angeles were "blacked out" during World War II, particularly good photographs of the Andromeda Galaxy could be taken because the sky was so dark. These showed for the first time that the stars near the nucleus of a spiral galaxy are all red giants, not at all like the "mixture" of young and old stars in the arms.

The 100-inch reflecting telescope on Mount Wilson, in California. Edwin Hubble (see page 114) used this telescope to work out the distance of the Andromeda Galaxy, and it also proved that the stars in the nucleus are all old red giants.

In 1885, a supernova explosion was seen in the Andromeda Galaxy. For a few nights a starlike point of light, easily visible without binoculars or a telescope, shone out as brightly as the whole galaxy of stars.

This shows the tremendous power of a supernova outburst, since the whole Andromeda Galaxy contains about 400 billion stars.

The far galaxies

After passing the edge of the Local Group, the next large spiral galaxies lie about eight million light-years away. Beyond this distance, more and more spiral, elliptical, and irregular galaxies come into view, but they appear smaller and fainter because they are so far away. Finally, at the very limit of the observable universe, a few very luminous galaxies, known as **quasars**, may be made out.

The more distant galaxies are not scattered in a haphazard way through space, but appear to form clusters. For example, there are many faint galaxies in the direction of the constellation Virgo. Distance measurements have shown that these galaxies, thousands of them, form a swarm in space about 60 million light-years away from the Milky Way Galaxy. They are known as the Virgo Cluster.

There are several other clusters of galaxies that can be seen with large telescopes. One, for example, is in the direction of the constellation Ursa Major. All these vast clusters, together with our own minute Local Group, seem to form a "supercluster" over 100 million light-years across, with a huge gulf of space before the next supercluster. Perhaps the whole universe is built up from superclusters of galaxies?

In the picture above, a jet of brilliant gas, thousands of light-years long, flares from the explosive nucleus of a huge elliptical galaxy.

This is how twin galaxies, eight and a half million light-years away, might appear if viewed from an intergalactic spacecraft.

Galaxies more than a few hundred million light-years away appear as faint smudges in our night sky. Those shown here belong to the largest supercluster known, which is seen in the constellation Hercules. It measures about 350 million light-years across, and is about 700 million light-years away.

The strange galaxies known as quasars are the most distant objects we know. They are about one hundred times brighter than the brightest galaxies found in our supercluster, and it seems likely that all this energy comes from a region of space equal to the diameter of Pluto's orbit, instead of from the whole galaxy.

If this is correct, a piece of a quasar's energy source just a half a mile across would give out as much heat and light as the Sun! If vast amounts of material at the center of the galaxy were falling into a "whirlpool" with a huge black hole at the center, this could possibly explain how so much energy is produced — but the quasars are still the most mysterious objects known in the universe.

This is how a quasar might look, if viewed from nearby. At the center of an elliptical galaxy, a brilliant point of light is surrounded by a spinning disk of shining material. The brilliance is believed to be caused by gas whirling faster and faster around a black hole until it is traveling almost at the speed of light.

Quasars seem to be huge but young galaxies that were formed soon after the birth of the universe. We only see them as young galaxies now because their light has taken billions of years to reach us on Earth.

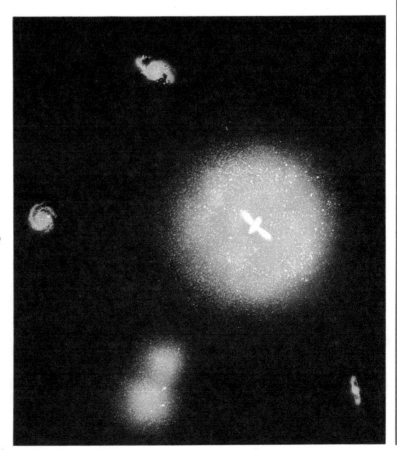

Probing the universe

How do we know that very distant galaxies and quasars really are all that far away? After all, they appear only as tiny specks on photographs taken with big telescopes, and it is impossible to see any details.

The credit for giving astronomers a "ruler" into the farthest depths of space belongs to the American astronomer Edwin Hubble, who lived in the first half of this century. He used the well-known fact that light travels in waves, and waves of blue light are much closer together than waves of red light.

Sound also travels in waves, and the higher the note, the shorter the sound waves. For example, if an ambulance drives past you very quickly, the noise of its siren seems to be lower when it has passed by, even though it is really the same. This is because the vehicle's speed has "stretched" out the sound waves behind it. In the same way, light rays that are sent out by an object speeding away from the Earth are also "stretched," making the object appear redder in color than if it was stationary. This appearance of change in color is known as the **red shift**.

Hubble's Law

Hubble made a careful study of galaxies, and discovered that the ones which appeared very small and faint (suggesting that they were far away) looked redder than the ones which he knew were nearer. Once he knew the distance of the nearer galaxies, he was able to work out the distances of the farther ones, just by measuring the difference in their color.

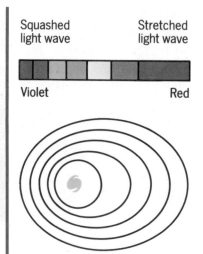

Squashed light wave Stretched light wave

Violet Red

A fast-moving object that gives out light "squashes" or "stretches" the light waves as it moves along. The object will look bluer to someone in front, and redder to someone behind.

The speeding ambulance shown below has the same effect on the sound waves it sends out. As it passes, the siren's note sounds lower, because the sound waves are "stretched" and produce a deeper note.

High notes (sound waves pushed together)

Low notes (sound waves pulled apart)

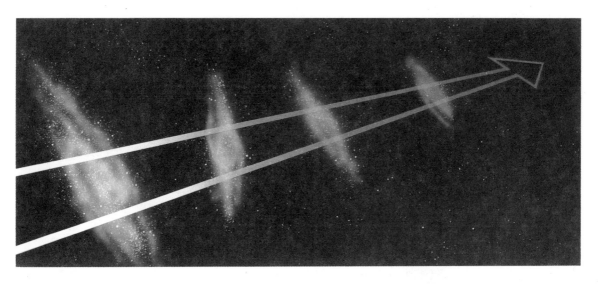

This method of measuring distances is known as Hubble's Law. It shows that some quasars are rushing away from our own Galaxy at speeds almost as great as the speed of light, which is as fast as anything in the universe can travel. The remotest known quasar, called PKS 2000–330, is about 15 billion light-years away, and is increasing its distance at a rate of about 155,000 miles (six times around the Earth) every second.

This means that we are seeing PKS 2000–330 as it appeared soon after the birth of the universe some 17 billion years ago. Our solar system did not even exist when the light now arriving in our telescopes left this object — and the brilliant energy source in the quasar must have died away long ago. What we are seeing now is a "ghost" from a long-vanished age.

Distant galaxies are moving outward at speeds of thousands of miles per second. This makes their light seem redder than it would if they were not moving. This change of color cannot be seen by the eye, but it can be detected using an instrument known as a "spectrograph." This turns a galaxy's light into a spectrum, so that the different colors can be measured.

THE SPECTRUM

When ordinary white light passes through a wedge-shaped piece of glass called a prism, the light is spread out into a colored band called the **spectrum**. The rainbow is a spectrum that forms when sunlight passes through raindrops.

The seven principal colors of the spectrum are shown here. All light is made up of light waves, but the distance between each wave, the "wavelength," is different for each color.

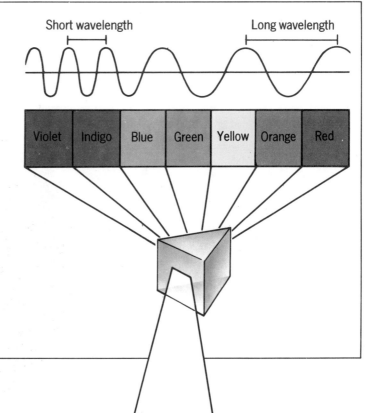

Short wavelength

Long wavelength

Violet Indigo Blue Green Yellow Orange Red

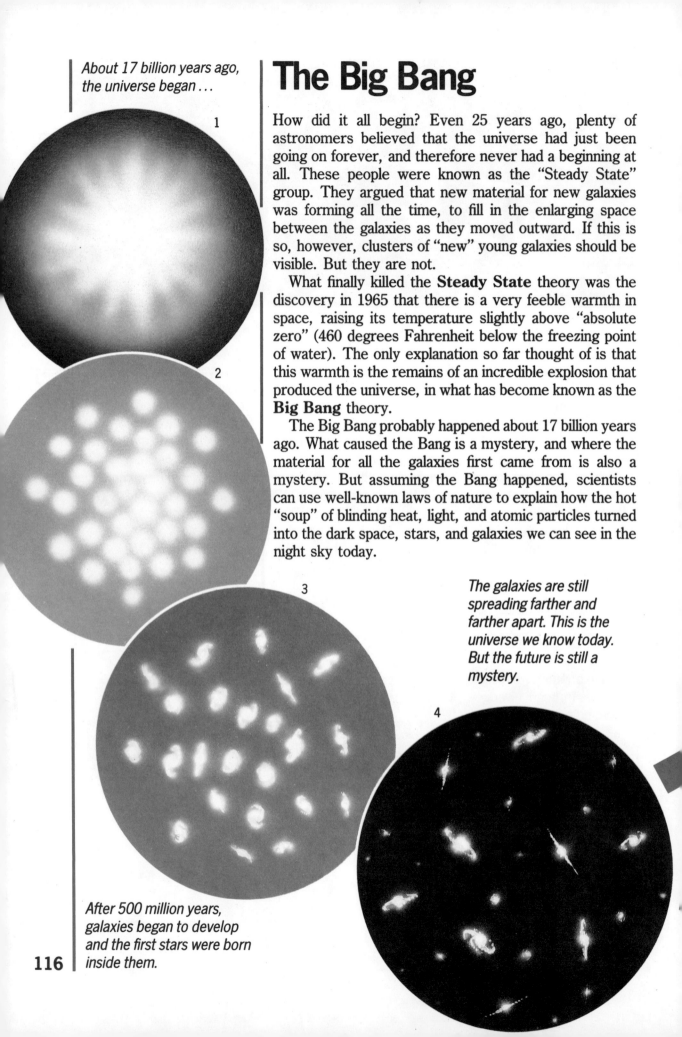

About 17 billion years ago, the universe began...

1

2

The Big Bang

How did it all begin? Even 25 years ago, plenty of astronomers believed that the universe had just been going on forever, and therefore never had a beginning at all. These people were known as the "Steady State" group. They argued that new material for new galaxies was forming all the time, to fill in the enlarging space between the galaxies as they moved outward. If this is so, however, clusters of "new" young galaxies should be visible. But they are not.

What finally killed the **Steady State** theory was the discovery in 1965 that there is a very feeble warmth in space, raising its temperature slightly above "absolute zero" (460 degrees Fahrenheit below the freezing point of water). The only explanation so far thought of is that this warmth is the remains of an incredible explosion that produced the universe, in what has become known as the **Big Bang** theory.

The Big Bang probably happened about 17 billion years ago. What caused the Bang is a mystery, and where the material for all the galaxies first came from is also a mystery. But assuming the Bang happened, scientists can use well-known laws of nature to explain how the hot "soup" of blinding heat, light, and atomic particles turned into the dark space, stars, and galaxies we can see in the night sky today.

3

The galaxies are still spreading farther and farther apart. This is the universe we know today. But the future is still a mystery.

4

After 500 million years, galaxies began to develop and the first stars were born inside them.

The end of the universe

Although distant galaxies seem to be flying away from our own Galaxy, this does not mean that we are at the "center" of the universe. Someone on a planet in one of these remote galaxies would see exactly the same thing — galaxies, including our own, flying away in all directions. The universe has no center, and no edge — it seems to go on forever.

But will it continue expanding forever? Or will the galaxies slow down, and even start collapsing inward again? The situation is a little like trying to launch a probe into space. If it is not given enough energy (in other words, it is not fired fast enough) it will eventually be slowed down by the Earth's gravity, and crash back onto the Earth's surface. But if it is given enough energy, it will break free of the Earth's gravity and soar off into space, never to return.

In the universe, the gravity trying to pull everything back together comes from all the galaxies or the superclusters of galaxies pulling at each other. If the Big Bang gave them enough of a flying start, their gravity will not be strong enough to slow them down and eventually pull them back together, and they will continue flying apart for all time. But if the explosion was not powerful enough, then they must already be slowing down, and billion of years into the future they will pull each other back into the ultimate collision — an event known as the **Big Crunch**.

The diagram below shows two ways in which the universe might continue.
1. In the "Never-ending" universe the galaxies will continue to fly apart until space is almost all black emptiness. Finally, the galaxies will die. Each of the stars will gradually fade away, until in a trillion years' time there will only be dead planets circling dead stars in utter blackness.
2. Alternatively, the galaxies may stop moving apart. Their gravity will then pull them inward again, closer and closer, until they collide and explode in a "Big Crunch." If this happens, perhaps another universe will be formed from the explosion, as our own may have been.

1. Never-ending universe

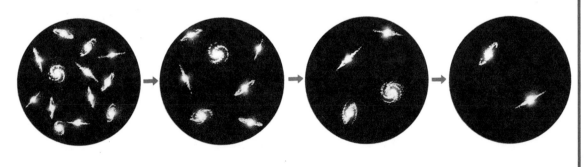

2. The Big Crunch

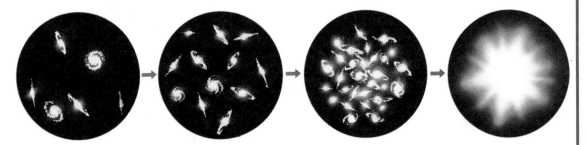

Life in the universe

If you asked someone to guess at all the living things that might be found in the sea simply by studying the tiny creatures found in a jar of seawater, it is not very likely that he or she would be able to imagine such things as sharks, or even shellfish. In trying to imagine what life-forms exist in the universe, we have the same problem — our "sample" of the universe is just too small to be helpful.

When the Viking spacecrafts took their life-hunting experiments to Mars in 1976, they made chemical tests on the Martian soil to see if the results were the same as the ones obtained using soil from the Earth, which contains living things. They were not, but this could just mean that living forms on Mars are different from ours.

All life-forms on the Earth are made up of cells built up from carbon atoms. The astronomer Fred Hoyle wrote a novel called *The Black Cloud*, about a "living" cloud of carbon atoms and other material floating through space. He showed how such a cloud might be able to receive radio signals sent to it from the Earth, and "learn" to decode and understand them. His story is fantasy, but no one has proved that this could not happen.

The upper levels of Jupiter, for example, are rich in substances made from carbon, nitrogen, and hydrogen, which might once have existed in the Earth's atmosphere when life began. The well-known American planetologist Carl Sagan is just one of several writers suggesting that these substances could have produced living cells, and finally creatures, which float in Jupiter's clouds.

There are many fantastic life-forms on the Earth's surface, but if living things exist on other planets they are almost certain to be more fantastic still. The picture above shows a biologist's idea of the kinds of floating and flying creatures that might be able to survive in Jupiter's upper clouds.

Some astronomers who have studied the Viking results sent back from the surface of Mars in 1976 feel that there could be living organisms in some less hostile places on the surface of Mars.

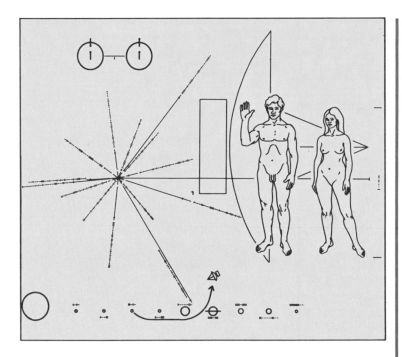

This metal panel is carried by Pioneer 10, which took close-up pictures of Jupiter in 1973 and could survive for billions of years as it drifts through the Galaxy.

In the faint hope that it may be rescued by some other intelligent life-form, the panel uses symbols to give some information about the Earth and the human race. The drawing along the bottom shows the solar system and the planet from which the spacecraft was sent.

Whether or not there is life elsewhere in the solar system, few people deny that intelligent life must exist elsewhere in the universe. But can we ever hope to communicate with it?

So far, no one has picked up radio signals from intelligent beings in space. When pulsars were first found (see page 90), there was a moment's excitement that the signals might be a message, but this was not the case.

Some people, however, have claimed that the Earth has already been visited by alien spacecrafts. In our turn, the space probe Pioneer 10 and the two Voyager crafts are carrying messages into space — just in case!

In the year A.D. 10,000,000, Voyager 2, battered by collisions with stray meteoroids, may drift into an alien solar system. What would happen if a strange spacecraft, also lost and drifting, was discovered in our solar system, perhaps heading toward the Earth?

Glossary

Andromeda Galaxy This is the closest GALAXY like our own. It belongs to the LOCAL GROUP. It is more than two million LIGHT-YEARS away, and there are about 400 billion stars in it.

Asteroid Another name for a minor planet — one of the thousands of small bodies circling around the Sun, measuring from a few yards to over 500 miles across.

Atmosphere The layer of gas around a planet. The Earth's atmosphere keeps us warm at night, and rain clouds can float in it. It also has oxygen for living organisms to breathe.

Atom The smallest "piece" of an ELEMENT. It contains PROTONS, NEUTRONS, and ELEC-TRONS. There are about a hundred trillion atoms in this period.

Aurora A display of colored light high in the Earth's ATMOSPHERE. It is caused when particles from the Sun make the gas in the atmosphere glow. This usually happens near the Earth's POLES.

Axis The imaginary line through the center of a spinning star or planet. Think of a pointed stick pushed through an orange and then spun like a top.

Big Bang The theory most astronomers use to explain how the UNIVERSE began. Everything that exists now was crushed into a superhot ball that exploded about 17 billion years ago.

Big Crunch What may happen in billions of years' time if the UNIVERSE collapses back again. But it is more likely to go on expanding forever.

Binary star A pair of stars turning around each other. They may take a few hours if they are very close, or thousands of years if they are far apart.

Black hole An object with such strong GRAVITY that LIGHT WAVES cannot escape from it. Anything pulled inside a black hole is lost forever.

Celestial sphere An imaginary hollow ball surrounding Earth that has the stars attached to it. It turns around us once a day, making the stars appear to rise and set in our sky.

Cepheids A special VARIABLE STAR. They change in brightness as their hot surfaces puff up and down. Bright Cepheids take longer to change than dimmer ones.

Comet A mixture of crumbly rock and ice a few miles across, which travels around the Sun. If it comes near the Sun the heat makes DUST and gas pour off in a long glowing "tail."

Comet

Constellation A group of stars making a pattern in the sky. Some constellations were named thousands of years ago. There are 88 covering the whole sky.

Corona The faint halo of DUST and gas above the Sun's bright surface. It can be seen during a total ECLIPSE of the Sun.

Crater The mark left when a small rocky body traveling around the Sun hits the surface of a solid planet or a moon and explodes.

Dust The name given to tiny particles, usually made of carbon, about a twenty-five thousandths of an inch across. These form huge dark NEBULAS in space.

Dwarf star Either an ordinary small dim star (red dwarf), or the dying remains of a bright star (white, brown, or black dwarf).

Eclipse When the Moon passes in front of the Sun and blocks its light from Earth (eclipse of the Sun), or the Moon passes into the Earth's shadow (eclipse of the Moon).

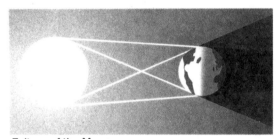
Eclipse of the Moon

Electron The part of an ATOM that spins around the solid center or "nucleus." Very hot atoms can lose electrons, and invisible clouds of electrons are sent into space by the Sun.

Elements Substances made of only one kind of ATOM. There are 92 different kinds of atoms, and therefore 92 different elements. Other substances are made of a mixture of elements.

Ellipse The shape of a planet's ORBIT as it spins around the Sun. The distance from the planet to the Sun varies as it moves once around its orbit.

Galaxy A "star city." It is where stars are born and die. Even a small galaxy contains several million stars — the largest may contain a trillion.

Giant stars May be either much hotter and brighter than the Sun (white or blue giants), or cool red stars that have puffed up to an enormous size (red giants).

Globules Round dark clouds of DUST and gas measuring about a LIGHT-YEAR across. These eventually turn into shining stars.

Gravity The mysterious pulling force that every object in the universe gives out. The larger the object the stronger its force of gravity.

Light waves A ray of light is made up of light waves. There are about 63,000 waves in every inch of blue light, and about 38,000 in every inch of red light. This means that each different light color has a different "wavelength."

Light-year The distance a ray of light travels through space in a year — about 5.9 trillion miles. Light is the fastest thing in the universe.

Local Group The collection of about 30 GALAXIES that includes our own Milky Way Galaxy. The largest member of the group is the ANDROMEDA GALAXY.

Magnetism A force found in planets, stars, and even whole galaxies. The huge amounts of iron at the center of the Earth cause the magnetic force that makes compass needles point north and south.

Magnitude The word an astronomer uses to describe the brightness of a star or planet. The smaller the magnitude number, the brighter it is.

Meteor The streak of light seen when a meteoroid — a particle between the size of a grain of sand and a pebble – burns up as it rushes into the ATMOSPHERE from space. Many meteoroids come from COMETS.

Meteorite The rocky or metallic remains of a meteoroid that hits the ground before it burns up. Not many are found, because most look like ordinary stones.

Meteorite

Milky Way The patchy band of pale light that circles the sky. It is hard to see from towns, but shines out in country skies. It is our view of our galaxy.

Moon or **satellite** A large natural object that orbits around a planet. The planet Saturn has 24 moons. Earth has only one natural moon, but thousands of artificial satellites also orbit our planet.

Nebula A huge cloud of DUST or gas, or a mixture of both. Some nebulas are many LIGHT-YEARS across. Nebulas are the birth-places of the stars. To begin with they are just cold dark patches, but when stars form inside them they can shine brightly.

Neutron A part of an ATOM. It is formed when an ELECTRON and a PROTON come together. The only atom that does not contain neutrons is the hydrogen atom.

Neutron star All that is left after a GIANT STAR explodes. It is completely made up of NEUTRONS, and these are crushed together into a hot ball the size of a small ASTEROID.

Nova A "new" star — really a very faint star that suddenly shines out thousands of times more brightly. This happens when gas passes from one star to another and explodes.

Orbit The invisible path that a planet follows around the Sun, or a satellite follows around a planet. Orbits are never perfect circles, but ELLIPSES.

Penumbra The lighter edge of a shadow, where the bright object (such as the Sun) is not completely hidden. It is also the name for the lighter edge of a SUNSPOT.

Phase The shape of the sunlit part of the Moon, or some planets, that is seen in the sky. It can change from a thin curved "crescent" to completely round or "full."

Photosphere The Sun's bright surface. Its temperature is 11,000 degrees Fahrenheit.

Poles The two opposite points on the surface of a spinning planet or star, where the AXIS passes through it.

Prominences Enormous bursts of red-hot hydrogen gas that shoot out from the Sun's surface. Some may last for weeks, others for days, before dying back to the surface.

Prominence

Protons Usually together with NEUTRONS, these make up the solid center of an ATOM. The number of protons is always the same as the number of ELECTRONS whirling around them.

Pulsar A fast-spinning NEUTRON STAR sending out a beam of light waves and radio waves. This beam makes a "pulse," like the circling beam of a lighthouse.

Quasars Giant GALAXIES with centers hundreds of times brighter than ordinary galaxies. They are all billions of LIGHT-YEARS away.

Red shift The color change shown by distant GALAXIES. They are moving away at thousands of miles a second, and their LIGHT WAVES are stretched out by the speed, making them look redder in color than they really are.

Rings Whirling bands of rock, ice, and dust found around the planets Jupiter, Saturn, and Uranus. They may have come from a nearby satellite that broke up.

Seasons Changes in the Earth's climate caused by the tilt of its AXIS. Each POLE leans toward the Sun for half the year, and away from the Sun for the other half. This brings summer and winter to each half of the Earth in turn.

Shooting star Another name for a METEOR.

Shooting stars

Solar system The family of planets, moons, and COMETS revolving around our Sun. There are probably countless other solar systems around stars in our GALAXY and elsewhere in the universe.

Solar wind An invisible stream of atomic particles, especially ELECTRONS and PROTONS, that pour out into space from the Sun's surface.

Spectrum The band of colors you see when light passes through a glass prism. A rainbow is a spectrum, produced by sunlight shining through raindrops.

Star cluster A group of stars containing from a few tens (an open cluster) up to hundreds of thousands (a globular cluster).

Steady State A theory of the UNIVERSE which says that ATOMS are being created all the time to make new GALAXIES, while the old ones fly apart. Most astronomers believe the BIG BANG theory, instead.

Sunspot A cool darker patch on the Sun's surface. Many sunspots are much bigger than the Earth.

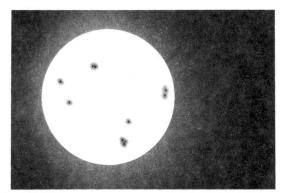

Sunspots

Sunspot cycle A period of time, lasting about 11 years, during which sunspots become very common (maximum activity) and then rare (minimum activity). The next "maximum" activity is due about 1990.

Supernova A colossal explosion that destroys a GIANT STAR. The outburst gives out as much light as billions of ordinary stars.

Tides These are caused by the force of GRAVITY of one body in space, pulling at the surface of a nearby body. The pull of our Moon causes tides in the oceans.

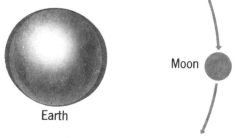

Moon

Earth

Tides

Transit When the inner planets, Mercury or Venus, pass in front of the Sun. They appear as a slow-moving black spot. Transits of Venus are very rare; the next one will be in the year 2004.

Umbra The dark center of a shadow, where all the light from the bright object is cut off. When the Moon passes into the umbra of Earth's shadow, it is ECLIPSED. It is also the name for the center of a SUN SPOT.

Universe The whole of space and everything in it. It has no "end" — however far you travel there will always be farther to go, just as you can never reach the "end" of a circle.

Variable star A star that changes in brightness. Some grow dimmer when a companion star passes in front of them. Others swell and shrink in size, and some explode as a NOVA or SUPERNOVA.

Zodiac An imaginary band around the CELESTIAL SPHERE. During a year, the Sun appears to travel along the center of this band. It passes through twelve Zodiacal CONSTELLATIONS.

Index

Page numbers in *italics* refer to pictures.

125

Acknowledgements

Pages: **2** © Kitt Peak National Observatory / Cerro Tololo Inter-American Observatory; **8** top right British Museum; **15** top left and top right National Optical Astronomy Observatories; **16** bottom Max Planck Institute for Radio Astronomy; **19** middle right NASA; **34** middle right Royal Astronomical Society; **36** bottom left Ann Ronan Picture Library; **48** middle left Royal Astronomical Society; **57** top right NASA; **58** middle right ZEFA; **63**, **65**, NASA; **67** top Kobal Collection, bottom NASA; **69** middle left NASA; **74** middle right Ann Ronan Picture Library; **76** bottom Anglo-Australian Telescope Board; **98** bottom Royal Observatory, Edinburgh; **99** California Institute of Technology and Carnegie Institute of Washington; **106** top Anglo-Australian Telescope Board; **108** top, **110** top California Institute of Technology and Carnegie Institute of Washington; **111** Ian Ridpath.